W9-BJE-267

DISCARD

HERMAN MELVILLE

EDITED AND WITH AN
INTRODUCTION BY HAROLD BLOOM

CURRENTLY AVAILABLE

BLOOM'S MAJOR NOVELISTS

Jane Austen
The Brontës
Willa Cather
Stephen Crane
Don DeLillo
Charles Dickens
Fyodor Dostoevsky
George Eliot
William Faulkner
F. Scott Fitzgerald
Thomas Hardy
Nathaniel Hawthorne
Ernest Hemingway
Henry James
James Joyce
Franz Kafka
D. H. Lawrence
Herman Melville
Toni Morrison
Marcel Proust
Thomas Pynchon
John Steinbeck
Stendhal
Leo Tolstoy
Mark Twain
Alice Walker
Edith Wharton
Virginia Woolf

HERMAN MELVILLE

EDITED AND WITH AN INTRODUCTION
BY HAROLD BLOOM

A Haights Cross Communications Company

Printed and bound in the United States of America.

First Printing
1 3 5 7 9 8 6 4 2

Library of Congress Cataloging-in-Publication Data
Herman Melville / edited and with an introduction by Harold Bloom.
p. cm. — (Bloom's major novelists)
Includes bibliographical references and index.
ISBN 0-7910-7027-1
1. Melville, Herman, 1819–1891—Criticism and interpretation. I. Bloom, Harold. II. Series.
PS2387 .H4 2002
813'.3—dc21

2002153645

Chelsea House Publishers
1974 Sproul Road, Suite 400
Broomall, PA 19008-0914

http://www.chelseahouse.com

Contributing Editor: Suzanne Barton Piorkowski

Cover design by Terry Mallon

Layout by EJB Publishing Services

CONTENTS

USER'S GUIDE

This volume is designed to present biographical, critical, and bibliographical information on the author and the author's best-known or most important works. Following Harold Bloom's editor's note and introduction is a concise biography of the author that discusses major life events and important literary accomplishments. A critical analysis of each novel follows, tracing significant themes, patterns, and motifs in the work. An annotated list of characters supplies brief information on the main characters in each novel.

A selection of critical extracts, derived from previously published material, follows each thematic analysis. In most cases, these extracts represent the best analysis available from a number of leading critics. Because these extracts are derived from previously published material, they will include the original notations and references when available. Each extract is cited, and readers are encouraged to use the original publications as they continue their research. A bibliography of the author's writings, a list of additional books and articles on the author and their work, and an index of themes and ideas conclude the volume.

As with any study guide, this volume is designed as a supplement to the works being discussed, and is in no way intended as a replacement for those works. The reader is advised to read the text prior to using this study guide, and to keep it accessible for quick reference.

ABOUT THE EDITOR

Harold Bloom is Sterling Professor of the Humanities at Yale University and Henry W. and Albert A. Berg Professor of English at the New York University Graduate School. He is the author of over 20 books, and the editor of more than 30 anthologies of literary criticism.

Professor Bloom's works include *Shelley's Mythmaking* (1959), *The Visionary Company* (1961), *Blake's Apocalypse* (1963), *Yeats* (1970), *A Map of Misreading* (1975), *Kabbalah and Criticism* (1975), *Agon: Toward a Theory of Revisionism* (1982), *The American Religion* (1992), *The Western Canon* (1994), and *Omens of Millennium: The Gnosis of Angels, Dreams, and Resurrection* (1996). *The Anxiety of Influence* (1973) sets forth Professor Bloom's provocative theory of the literary relationships between the great writers and their predecessors. His most recent books include *Shakespeare: The Invention of the Human*, a 1998 National Book Award finalist, *How to Read and Why* (2000), and *Genius: A Mosiac of One Hundred Exemplary Creative Minds* (2002).

Professor Bloom earned his Ph.D. from Yale University in 1955 and has served on the Yale faculty since then. He is a 1985 MacArthur Foundation Award recipient and served as the Charles Eliot Norton Professor of Poetry at Harvard University in 1987–88. In 1999 he was awarded the prestigious American Academy of Arts and Letters Gold Medal for Criticism. Professor Bloom is the editor of several other Chelsea House series in literary criticism, including BLOOM'S MAJOR SHORT STORY WRITERS, BLOOM'S MAJOR NOVELISTS, BLOOM'S MAJOR DRAMATISTS, BLOOM'S MODERN CRITICAL INTERPRETATIONS, BLOOM'S MODERN CRITICAL VIEWS, and BLOOM'S BIOCRITIQUES.

EDITOR'S NOTE

My Introduction meditates upon Captain Ahab as Promethean Gnostic quester, representative of Melville's own Gnostic knowing.

All eleven of the Critical Views on *Moby Dick* are genuinely useful, so I will indicate here only a few of particular interest to me. Paul Brodtkorb, Jr. invokes the historical psychology of J. H. Van Den Berg as intellectual context for Ishmael-as-narrator.

Shakespearean influence, crucial upon Ahab, is memorably explored by Charles Olson and by P. Adams Sitney. The homoerotic element in *Moby Dick* is examined by Leo Bersani, while Bainard Cowan analyzes Shakespearean foreshadowings, and William B. Dillingham expounds the thematic of martyrdom.

The highly problematical *Pierre* receives eight helpful views, including Edward H. Rosenberry and Edgar A. Dryden on Shakespeare's presence in the novel. Dean Richard H. Brodhead gives a distinguished analysis of Melville's modes in creating *Pierre*.

The eight excerpts upon the enigma of *The Confidence Man* all help illuminate a dark work. A debate about "faith" in the novel is conducted by Hershel Parker, James Duban, Clark Davis, and Joyce Sparer Adler.

Daniel G. Hoffman broods on the relation of *The Confidence Man* to Melville's society, after which Helen P. Trimpi ventures an interpretation of the book's meanings, and Tom Quirk concludes with estimating Melville's vision of character in this novel.

INTRODUCTION

Harold Bloom

There are three nineteenth century prime candidates for the American epic: *Moby-Dick*, *Song of Myself*, and *Adventures of Huckleberry Finn*. If the twentieth century adds a fourth candidate, it might be Thomas Pynchon's *Mason & Dixon* or Cormac McCarthy's *Blood Meridian*, unless one puts together Faulkner's complex saga by excerpting from a number of works, as Malcolm Cowley did in his *Portable Faulkner*. Given a vote, I would select *Moby-Dick*, though the total Walt Whitman seems to me our national writer, with Ralph Waldo Emerson the only possible rival.

Melville the novelist is hardly a one-book man: *Pierre*, though a failure, is a sublime one, and *The Confidence-Man* and *Billy Budd* are remarkable in very different ways. Since Melville at his best was a strong poet, and his *Piazza Tales* are marvelous, the overall achievement fascinates. Nevertheless *Moby-Dick* is unique within the Melville canon, and still a permanent splendor both in American and world literature.

This influence of Shakespeare and of Cervantes is marked and overt in *Moby-Dick*, but the presence of Melville's major precursors does not limit the majesty or the originality. I once found myself affirming that Ahab both was and was *not* a hero-villain on two consecutive pages of a book I had written. My self-contradiction carried me back to childhood, when I identified with the *Pequod's* obsessed captain, and forward to old age, when I shudder at the consequences of Ahab's quest. Like Macbeth, Ahab provokes our ambivalences.

But I do not think that Melville is equivocal about Ahab. How can a writer (unless he is Shakespeare) distance himself from a protagonist as urgent as Ahab?

> If man will strike, strike through the mask! How can the prisoner reach outside except by thrusting through the wall? To me, the white whale is that wall, shoved near me. Sometimes I think there's naught beyond. But 'tis enough. He tasks me; he heaps me; I see in him outrageous strength, with an inscrutable

> malice sinewing it. That inscrutable thing is chiefly what I hate; and be the white whale agent, or be the white whale principal, I will wreak that hate upon him. Talk not to me of blasphemy, man; I'd strike the sun if it insulted me.

How different are the two uses of "strike"! To strike through the mask is to defy one's own nihilism, but to strike the sun is to refuse acknowledgement that we are here to be insulted. Melville's *Pequod* is Quaker-owned, but Starbuck is the only Quaker, indeed the only Christian, on board. Ahab has gone from Quakerism to pure Zoroastrianism and ends as a Promethean Gnostic. Ishmael, the narrator, is an Emersonian Platonist, and the rest of the crew are animists, Zoroastrian dualists, atheists, or sublime idol-worshippers like Queequeg.

Ishmael is one of the most problematic narrators in all of literature. We are told that "Ahab's Ahab," a firm identity, but Ishmael is and is not Melville, is and is not Ahab, and Starbuck wonders whether Ahab is Ahab. Confronted by Moby-Dick, at once Leviathan and Behemoth, do we not all become Job? Under Melville's influence, Ralph Ellison's Invisible Man will fuse Jonah and Job, but the fusion exists already in Ishmael/Melville.

Ahab's father, he says, is the Demiurge, the false creator-god (or botcher) of this cosmos, but Ahab favors his mother, the abyss, which preceded our cosmological emptiness. Ishmael, a wonder-wounded auditor of Ahab, despite his sense of Ahab's greatness, seems closer to Emerson's Platonism than to Ahab's Gnosticism. The immense beauty of Melville's novel comes to us through Ishmael, who perhaps represents the poet in Melville more than the novelist. Ishmael has a real touch of Shakespearean detachment in him, but Ahab is about as detached as King Lear was.

Huck Finn and "Walt Whitman" move us to poignant affection, while Ahab seems beyond our capacity to absorb him. Faulkner's Ahabian heroes are not on Melville's huge scale. Ahab remains still the tragic version of the American hero, epic in scope, doom-eager always.

BIOGRAPHY OF

Herman Melville

Herman Melville was born the third of eight children in New York City on August 1, 1819 to Allan and Maria Ganesvoort Melvill. Melville's family boasted strong patriotic roots with his two grandfathers having played pivotal roles in America's fight for freedom. His paternal grandfather took part in the Boston Tea Party, while his maternal grandfather was a general in the Revolutionary War.

Financial stability became a problem early on in Melville's life, and would prove to be a seemingly endless nuisance. Although initially well-off, Melville's father, an importer and commission merchant, over-extended himself financially. In 1830, when Herman was twelve, the family moved from New York City to Albany where Allan would try his luck in the fur business. This venture failed, after which Allan Melvill died of a sudden illness in 1832. Allan's death marked a big change for a family that was once accustomed to the comforts of wealth. The Melvill's were forced to rely upon the financial support of relatives, and young Herman took a job as a bank clerk to help support his family. It was around this time that Herman's family altered the spelling of its name by adding an "e" to the end. While working, Melville was able to attend some school and he read a great deal. Even without a formal education, he was able to obtain a job teaching in rural Massachusetts. However, the remoteness of the one-room schoolhouse and the hodgepodge of students seeking an education proved too much for the first time educator. He returned home after a month, once again looking for employment. After being turned down for a job working on the reconstruction of the Erie Canal, Melville and a friend traveled to Illinois hoping to find work with Melville's uncle Thomas. When the journey did not result in a job, Melville found his way back east after traveling the Mississippi, and decided to try working at sea. He got a job as a cabin boy on a ship hauling cotton to Liverpool, England. He enjoyed the work, but was affected by the poverty he encountered in the slums of the port city. This experience in England shaped both his writing and his politics.

After his adventure as a cabin boy, Melville once again tried his hand at teaching, and once more was unsuccessful—the school ran out of money before the end of the school year. Melville's struggles with earning a living continued to beleaguer him.

Melville's next move greatly influenced his writing career when in 1841 he signed up for a job on the whaling ship *Acushnet* and headed for the South Seas. Accounts of Melville's travels through present-day French Polynesia vary, and are most likely embellished, but it is reported that he and a friend jumped ship some time in July of that year. It is around this time that Melville reportedly spent time with the cannabilistic Typee people. This adventure would be the basis for his first and one of his most successful novels—*Typee*. By August, he was registered as part of the crew on an Australian whaler, the *Lucy Ann*. This adventure ended when he was jailed for participating in a mutiny. In November he signed up as a harpooner on the *Charles & Henry*—his third and final whaling trip. Six months later, he disembarked in Hawaii where he eventually joined the crew of the frigate *United States*. On October 3, 1844, Melville and the rest of the crew arrived at the Boston Navy Yard.

Melville returned to a much more prosperous family as his brother Gansevoort had become a well-respected lawyer and politician. Encouraged by his family to record his travels, Melville began writing. His first novel *Typee*, published in 1846, was a fictionalized account of his time in the South Pacific, and was generally well received by the public. His second book *Omoo* continued his adventures on the tropical islands of the Pacific Ocean. Both books were critical and commercial successes, but questions were raised about the accuracy of the works. In 1847, he married Elizabeth Shaw—the couple would have four children together. Living with his mother and four sisters, Melville set himself to the task of supporting his family through his writing. His next book *Mardi* did not do as well as he had hoped, but in his subsequent works *Redburn* and *White-Jacket*, he returned to the style that his readers enjoyed.

In 1851 Herman Melville published his best-known work, *Moby-Dick*, though at the time it brought him neither fame nor fortune. *Redburn* and *White-Jacket* were a return to the style present in *Typee*, but it was Melville's friendship with writer Nathaniel Hawthorne that provided the invigorating spark for Melville's imagination. Melville's next book was the vastly different, and financially disappointing *Pierre* (1852), after which he enjoyed some success with *Israel Potter* (1855). During the years between 1853 and 1855 Melville contributed several short stories ("Bartleby the Scrivener," "The Encantadas," and "Benito Cereno") to Putnam's Monthly Magazine. All of these stories reflected Melville's increasing disfavor of materialism.

After writing ten books in ten years, and having become more secluded during that time, Melville traveled to Europe in 1856. Upon his returned, Melville wrote *The Confidence Man*, published in 1857. This novel would be the last to be published in Melville's lifetime.

No longer able to support his family with his writing, Melville undertook three American lecture tours, after which he attempted his final sea voyage—a trip with his brother Thomas around Cape Horn. Melville quit the trip in San Francisco. By 1863, the family moved back to New York City, where Melville took a job as a customs inspector for New York Harbor—a job he held for nearly 20 years. This position, and an inheritance from his wife's father, allowed Melville a modicum of financial comfort. During this period, Melville still found time to write, and focused his efforts on poetry and more short stories.

In 1867 Melville suffered the death of his oldest son Malcolm who shot himself, perhaps accidentally, after a dispute with Melville. Tragedy struck again in 1886 when Melville's second son Stanwix died from tuberculosis at the age of 35.

After retiring from his job as a customs inspector, Melville continued to write—publishing more poetry and working on a novel. He died in New York City on September 28, 1891, all but forgotten as a writer—the New York Times printed his obituary as "Henry Melville."

Melville's works began gaining popularity in the 1920s. A student reviewing some of Melville's papers uncovered the short novel *Billy Budd*. When published 33-years after Melville's death, it sparked an interest in Melville's works that continues today.

PLOT SUMMARY OF

Moby-Dick

"Call me Ishmael" is the reader's first introduction to the narrator of *Moby-Dick* as he relates his attraction, and in fact all man's attraction, to the sea. Ishmael's justification mimicks Melville's reasons for going to sea: "having little or no money in my purse, and nothing in particular to interest me on shore, I thought I would sail about a little and see the watery part of the world." The novel, concerned primarily with the journey of the whaling vessel *Pequod*, prefaced by Ishmael's story of joining the *Pequod*, and interspersed with extensive discourse on whaling, is also the story of humanity. Rich in symbols and themes, *Moby-Dick* juxtaposes ideas such as civilization and savagery, free will and determination, lightness and darkness, science and superstition, and Christianity and paganism among others.

The early part of the novel acquaints the reader with Ishmael, who is instantly confronted with bad luck as he misses the boat to Nantucket. Rejecting two inns as being too expensive, Ishmael settles on a third, the Spouter Inn, run by landlord Peter Coffin. Informed that there are no spare beds, Ishmael is given the option to share a bed with a harpooner—currently out trying to sell his last New Zealand embalmed head. The harpooner's return to the inn is the reader's and Ishmael's introduction to the cannibal Queequeg. This scene is both tense and humorous as Queequeg, covered in tattoos, performs idol worship and smokes from a tomahawk shaped pipe before unsuspectingly jumping into bed with his new bedmate. Later, as the two explore New Bedford, they form a fast friendship despite their difficulties in communicating with each other.

While exploring, Ishmael attends a Whaleman's Chapel Sunday service conducted by former harpooner Father Mapple. The father's sermon retells the story of Jonah and the Whale, and emphasizes the importance of belief in "the Lord his God." As Queequeg and Ishmael become friends, it is important to note that it is Queequeg and not Father Mapple that turns Ishmael towards goodness: "No more my splintered heart and maddened hand were turned against the wolfish world. This soothing savage had redeemed it."

Ishmael and Queequeg then travel to Nantucket together to sign on to a Whaler ship. While journeying to Nantucket aboard the *Moss*, a young sailor is swept overboard, and Queequeg dives in to rescue him—the first of three instances in which Queequeg rescues someone from drowning. Three proves to be a significant number throughout the novel with The Spouter Inn being the third inn Ishmael considers back in New Bedford. Once in Nantucket, Ishmael considers three ships before deciding on the third ship, the *Pequod*.

Ishmael ventures out to meet the two investors in the *Pequod* who are in charge of preparing the ship for voyage, Nantucket Quakers Bildad and Peleg. Ishmael accepts his position on the ship, and promises to bring Queequeg by the following day. Although initially opposed to hiring the pagan, Bildad and Peleg are convinced by Queequeg's accuracy with a harpoon, and Ishmael's insistence that Queequeg is no pagan, but is instead a member of the "whole worshipping world's" church. It is here through Peleg that Ishmael learns of the sick captain Ahab whose leg was chewed by a whale. Shortly after taking leave of Bildad and Peleg, the two men encounter the strange sailor Elijah who also warns of the tormented captain Ahab. It is a cold Christmas morning when the *Pequod* leaves Nantucket.

The interlude before the real voyage begins, "The Lee Shore" (chapter 23), has Ishmael contemplating man's restlessness, and concluding "in landlessness alone resides highest truth." Much of the following chapters work to introduce the remaining main characters: the cautious first-mate Starbuck; the easy-going second-mate Stubb and the quick to anger and fearless Flask. When Ahab finally appears, Ishmael describes him as "a man cut away from the stake, when the fire has overrunningly wasted all the limbs without consuming them, or taking away one particle from their compacted aged robustness." He later continues:

> So powerfully did the whole grim aspect of Ahab affect me, and the livid brand which streaked it, that for the first few moments I hardly noted that not a little of this overbearing grimness was owing to the barbaric white leg upon which he partly stood. It had previously come to me that this ivory leg

had at sea been fashioned from the polished bone of the sperm whale's jaw.

Ahab's first visit on deck proved brief, after which he makes regular appearances on deck every day, becoming more genial as the weather improved.

The following chapters are interspersed with Ishmael's reflections on whaling, defending the profession as honorable and necessary. Chapter 32, "Cetology," has Ishmael classifying whales according to both whaling lore and the zoology of the time—citing the sperm whale as "without doubt, the largest inhabitant of the globe; the most formidable of all whales to encounter."

It isn't until Chapter 36, "The Quarter-Deck," that Ahab's intentions to exact revenge on the great white whale are revealed. Moby Dick comes to symbolize the supernatural powers that have insulted Ahab, while at the same time being the very real whale responsible for the loss of Ahab's leg. Ahab then nails a gold doubloon to the mast promising it to the first man who spots the White Whale. To further guarantee the crew's allegiance, the sailors participate in a ritualistic drinking from the harpoon sheaths of Ahab's three harpooners and swear, "God hunt us all, if we do not hunt Moby Dick to his death!"

Chapters 37, 38, and 39 are soliloquies for Ahab, Starbuck and Stubb respectively. Ahab considers himself "damned in the midst of Paradise!" as his soliloquy continues the contrast between lightness and darkness. Starbuck, who hates and pities Ahab, feels trapped, and wrestles with succumbing to Ahab's plans: "My soul is more than matched; she's over-manned; and by a madman!"

The next couple of chapters provide information on Moby Dick, and explanations for his whiteness. It is here that the legend of the great whale is explained. He is considered the most perilous whale of the seas, and some have attributed his assaults to a malignant intelligence. Others consider him to be immortal, having survived many wounds. As to his whiteness, Ishmael says, "It was the whiteness of the whale that above all things appalled me." Chapter 42, "The Whitness of the Whale," is Ishmael's discussion of the various symbolic meanings of the color white.

"The Mat-Maker," chapter 47, has Queequeg and Ishmael weaving a sword-mat used to protect the ships riggings. Ishmael uses this opportunity to see the weaving as a metaphor for life. In it he views the fixed threads as fate, and the cross-threads as his own destiny weaving its way through fate: "This warp seemed necessity; and here, thought I, with my own hand I ply my own shuttle and weave my own destiny into these unalterable threads." Finally Qeequeg's "impulsive, indifferent sword, sometimes hitting the woof slantingly, or crookedly, or strongly, or weakly" is viewed as chance acting upon both free will and necessity. The weaving however, is interrupted by the sighting of a whale, the commotion of which brings the appearance of "dark Ahab, who was surrounded by five dusky phantoms that seemed fresh formed out of air."

The five men, with their leader Fedallah, were brought on board to man Ahab's whaleboat. They are described as "tiger yellow creatures," who, "seemed all steel and whalebone." During the first whale-chase, Queequeg's harpoon grazes a whale, but the ship he is in (along with Starbuck and Ishmael) is swamped. Unable to hail the other boats, the men in Starbuck's boat spend the night out at sea. The following morning, Starbuck's crew is surprised when the *Pequod* emerges from the morning mist, nearly killing them as it crushes their boat underneath.

One night, several weeks later (chapter 51), Fedallah spots the silvery jet of a whale believed to be Moby Dick. This scene provide the first glimpse of Ahab's maniacal pacing, "Walking the deck with quick, side-lunging strides, Ahab commanded the t'gallant sails and royals to be set, and every stunsail spread.... While his one live leg made lively echoes along the deck, every stroke of his dead limb sounded like a coffin-tap."

As the *Pequod* continues its journey, it encounters a homeward-bound Nantucket ship, the *Goney*. Ahab, who seldom socializes with other ship captains unless for news of Moby Dick, asks, "Have ye seen the white Whale?" The weather conspired against the two ships meeting and the *Goney* continued its course sailing away from the *Pequod*. Later, a second homeward-bound Nantucket ship, the *Town-Ho*, reports strong news of Moby Dick, but Ishmael instead relates the story of this ship as he once told it to friends in Lima.

After several chapters in which Ishmael considers the various depictions of whales (chapters 55–57), Daggoo cries out at what he perceives to be the White Whale. The boats are lowered once again, but only to discover the white mass to be a giant squid. A day after the squid sighting, as Queequeg had predicted "'When you see him 'quid,' said the savage, honing his harpoon in the bow of his hoisted boat, 'then you quick see him 'parm whale,'" Ishmael and the rest of the crew spot a sperm whale and give chase. In a gruesome description (chapter 61), Stubb kills the whale, after which it is lashed to the *Pequod*. Chapter 64, "Stubb's Supper," has Stubb dining on whale steak, while sharks tear away at the carcass drawing a poignant comparison between the voracious appetites of man and shark alike.

In chapters 67 through 70, Ishmael recounts the cutting of the whale, the releasing of the carcass, and Ahab's questioning of the sphinx-like whale head. The *Pequod* then meets the *Jeraboam*, whose captain refuses any contact between the two ship's crews.

With the sperm whale's head still attached to the ship, Ahab orders the crew to hunt the inferior right whale. Upon killing a right whale, Flask and Stubb consider Ahab's intentions with Flask saying "'did you never hear that the ship which but once has a Sperm Whale's head hoisted on her starboard side, and at the same time a Right Whale's on the larboard; did you never hear, Stubb, that that ship can never afterwards capsize?'" While harvesting the spermaceti from the newly acquired whale head, Tashtego falls overboard, only to be saved by Queequeg—his second rescue.

The next ship the *Pequod* encounters is the *Jungfrau* (Virgin). After supplying the *Jungfrau* with oil, the two ships compete for the largest of eight whales, with the *Pequod*'s harpooners striking first. Even though the whale is killed, he sinks instead of floating—foreshadowing the *Pequod*'s ill fate.

As the ship continues through sperm whale cruising grounds, Ishmael notes Ahab's refusal to touch land, keeping the crew constantly at sea. When near Java Head, the *Pequod* gives chase to a herd of whales, and is itself chased for a spell by Malayan pirates. Once safely away from the pirates, and still pursuing the whales, the boats are lowered and surrounded by the herd. Darting and wounding many, they manage to kill only one.

One or two weeks later the *Pequod* encounters the French whaler *Bouton de Rose* (Rose-bud) amid the stench of dead whales. The French, not known for their prowess as whalers are also the first ship with no news of Moby Dick.

Chapter 93 bears witness to Pip's transformation. Pip, who

usually stays on board as the boats give chase, is pressed into service on Stubb's boat. During Pip's second outing on the boat, the darted whale gave Pip such a start that he jumped overboard and became entagled in the whale line—forcing the line to be cut, and the whale to be lost. On Pip's next outing, despite Stubb's advice to "stick to the boat," Pip again jumped, and this time was left behind. Left to manage the sea by himself for some time, Pip was traumatized by the experience. Ishmael notes, "The sea had jeeringly kept his finite body up, but drowned the infinite of his soul," and although rescued, Pip "went about the deck an idiot."

In a bit of foreshadowing, while Ishmael squeezes lumps from the spermaceti, and in so doing feels cleansed of his oath against Moby Dick. He inadvertently squeezes the hands of his fellow crewmen, and upon looking into their eyes sees, "long rows of angels in paradise, each with his hands in a jar of spermaceti." This image is followed by the image of the try-works at night replete with hellish connotations. Harpooners gesticulating "with their huge pronged forks and dippers; as the wind howled on, and the sea leaped, and the ship groaned and dived, and yet steadfastly shot her red hell further and further into the blackness of the sea and the night." The *Pequod* is described as "frightened with savages, and laden with fire."

In chapter 100, the *Pequod* meets the *Samuel Enderby*, and English ship whose captain Boomer lost his arm to the great White Whale. Unlike Ahab, Boomer refuse to chase the whale asking, "ain't one limb enough?"

After several digressions about whales and whale bones, Ishmael recounts the scene in which Ahab splinters his ivory leg. Ahab then meets with the carpenter as he fashions a new leg for the captain. Starbuck then approaches Ahab, (chapter 109), who informs the captain that the oil in the hold is leaking. Ahab, more concerned with hunting the White Whale, refuses Starbuck's request to find and fix the leak. Starbuck, however, persists in his demands. Ahab, enraged, points a loaded musket at Starbuck's chest and commands, "'There is one God that is Lord over the earth, and one Captain that is lord over the Pequod.—On deck!' " Starbuck obeys, but warns Ahab to beware of Ahab.

After this brief skirmish, Ahab concedes and orders the hold to be searched. During the search, Queequeg crawls about in the belly of the ship, and falls gravely ill. He asks that a canoe/coffin be made out of dark wood, as he shuddered at the thought of being wrapped in his hammock and tossed overboard like refuse. Once the coffin is made, Qeequeg asks to be lifted from his hammock and placed inside so that he might see what comforts, if any, it afforded. Yet shortly after trying his coffin out, Queequeg recovers saying, "he had just recalled a little duty ashore, which he was leaving undone; and therefore had changed his mind about dying: he could not die yet, he averred."

In the Pacific, Ahab has the blacksmith forge a barb-ended harpoon from old horse-shoe stubbs, "the best and stubbornest stuff we blacksmiths ever work." Then in yet another dark ritual, Ahab tempers the barb with the blood from the three pagan harpooners, and baptizes it in the name of the devil.

The next ship the *Pequod* encounters is the *Bachelor*, a jolly ship bursting at the seems with whale oil. The two ships cross paths with no news of Moby Dick. After this encounter, four whales are killed, one of them by Ahab. As Ahab and his boat stay by the whale's side until they can be picked up by the *Pequod*, the Parsee, Fedallah, repeats three prophecies to Ahab: that "neither hearse nor coffin" can be Ahab's; that Ahab will not die until he sees two hearses "the first not made by mortal hands; and the visible wood of the last one must be grown in America"; and that Fedallah must go before Ahab as his pilot. Ahab takes these predictions to mean that he will succeed in slaying Moby Dick, and Fedallah retorts, "Hemp only can kill thee." Ahab takes this last prediction to mean that he can only be killed at the gallows, and claims himself immortal.

Chapter 119, "The Candles," has the *Pequod* hit by a typhoon head-on. Here the three masts catch fire and chaos ensues. Seeing the white flames, Ahab speaks, "the white flame but lights the way to the White Whale!" When Starbuck sees Ahab's barbed harpoon ablaze, he implores Ahab, "God, God is against thee, old man; forbear! 'tis an ill voyage! ill begun, ill continued; let me square the yards, while we may, old man, and make a fair wind of it homewards, to go on a better voyage than this." Ahab will have none of this, and grabbing the flaming harpoon threatens to lance any one who tries to strike the sails.

As the storm abates, Starbuck goes below deck to apprise Ahab of the situation on deck, and in this moment contemplates killing Ahab with the very musket that Ahab had once pointed at Starbuck. Despite sensing a kindred spirit in and adopting the mad Pip, Ahab locks him in his cabin, fearing that Pip might cure him of his monomania.

The *Pequod* then meets the ship *Rachel*. The captain of *Rachel*, has indeed seen Moby Dick, and lost a son at sea during the chase—Ahab refuses to help in the search. After this, the *Pequod* meets one last ship, a miserable ship named the *Delight*. The day before, the *Delight* lost five men to Moby Dick, all but one buried at sea. When the corpse of the fifth sailor is dropped overboard, the *Pequod* is sprayed in a sort of reverse baptism.

During a calm interlude, Ahab opens up a bit to Starbuck, lamenting the unfairness of his leg. He says, "I feel deadly faint, bowed, and humped, as though I were Adam, staggering beneath the piled centuries since Paradise."

The last chapters tell of three chases of Moby Dick. On the first encounter, the whale bites Ahab's boat in half. The second time the boats are lowered, Moby Dick becomes entangled in harpoons and takes the boats of Stubb and Flask underwater. He also flips Ahab's boat (a spare), tossing the crew into the air, and disappears. Several men are wounded, Ahab's leg is again splintered, and he has lost his special harpoon. When the crew reassembles on the deck of the *Pequod*, they realize that Fedallah is missing—perhaps his prophecy fulfilled. Here Ahab unwittingly declares things that are drowning rise twice, but sink forever the third time, as the carpenter makes him a third leg.

On the third day, Ahab shouts against the wind, declaring himself nobler than the "nobel and heroic" wind. The boats are lowered, and the sharks follow Ahab's boat only. Moby Dick smashes Stubb's and Flask's boats, and Fedallah's body is seen strapped by a reel line to the body of Moby Dick—the hearse not made by mortal hands. The crew of the two destroyed boats is ordered back to the *Pequod*, leaving Ahab to chase the whale alone. Moby Dick tips Ahab's boat, and all but one man makes it back on board. The whale then snaps the line, and proceeds to attack the *Pequod*. As the ship begins to sink Ahab realizes another of Fedallah's prophecies—the man-made hearse of American wood that cannot be his. Ahab darts Moby Dick for the last time, as the line (the hemp of Fedallah's prophecy) catches him around the neck and he is pulled underwater. As the *Pequod* sinks, the vortex created by the ship pulls Ahab's boat and its crew under.

The **epilogue** has Ishmael describing how he was the sole survivor. He had replaced Fedallah on Ahab's ship, and was the man who couldn't make it back to the ship. Queequeg's former coffin rose from the sunken ship, and Ishmael clings to it for a day until he is rescued by the *Rachel* (thus Queequeg saves a life for a third time). The *Rachel* still searching "only found another orphan."

LIST OF CHARACTERS IN
Moby-Dick

Ishmael is the narrator of the novel. He is a sailor who signed up for his first whaling journey. He tells the story of the ill-fated *Pequod* and the conflict caused by its Captain's obsession with the legendary white whale. He provides many insights into the business of whaling and about whales.

Ahab is Captain of the *Pequod*. He has been a whaler all his life. On his last whaling trip, he encountered Moby Dick, the white whale, who bit off his leg. The novel follows Ahab's monomaniacal quest to kill Moby Dick.

Starbuck is the first mate on board the *Pequod*. He is the only member of the crew remotely defiant of Ahab. He is a religious man, but avoids confronting troublesome questions. He is also practical and understands the whale ship's mission is to make money for its owners.

Stubb is the second mate on board the *Pequod*. His personality is optimistic and generally easy going. He is neither reflective nor afraid of death.

Flask is the third mate on board the *Pequod*. He is fearless, and becomes angry easily.

Queequeg is a harpooner on the *Pequod*. He and Ishmael meet in Nantucket before signing up for a whaling trip. While the tattooed savage initially frightens Ishmael, the two become great friends. Queequeg represents the noble savage, challenging conventional ideas of what it means to be civilized.

Fedallah (the Parsee) is a dark figure from Persia and is Ahab's harpooner. He makes several prophecies concerning Ahab's fate. He is a mystery to many on board the ship, and represents the shadow that Ahab's soul has created.

Pippin, better known as **'Pip'** by everyone on board the *Pequod*, becomes an oarsman on Stubb's whaleboat. He becomes frightened during the hunt for a whale and jumps overboard. Stubb fishes him out, but warns Pip if it happens again, he will leave him at sea. When he jumps ship again, he is left in the ocean, and picked up after a day. This traumatic experience causes his madness. Ahab takes pity on him, and he represents the goodness Ahab's soul has lost.

Tashtego, an Indian from Martha's Vineyard, is Stubb's harpooner. Queequeg saves him from drowning.

Dagoo is a large pagan from Africa, and is the harpooner on Flask's whaleboat.

Fleece is the old black cook on board the *Pequod*. Stubb makes him preach to a school of sharks.

Dough Boy is the steward of the Pequod. While nervous around the 'savage' harpooners, he serves dinner to the crew of the ship.

Perth is the blacksmith on board who puts together Ahab's harpoon, made especially for Moby Dick.

The ship's **Carpenter** is called upon to make a new leg for Ahab, and a coffin for Queequeg. The coffin survives the sinking of the *Pequod* and keeps Ishmael afloat until he is rescued.

Father Mapple is a famous preacher and former harpooner who Ishmael listens to before setting sail. Mapple gives a colorful sermon on 'Jonah and the Whale.'

Peleg and **Bildad** are two investors in the *Pequod*, and are in charge of outfitting the ship.

Elijah is a former sailor who torments Ishmael and Queequeg with foreboding prophecies about Ahab and the voyage.

CRITICAL VIEWS ON

Moby-Dick

Alfred Kazin on Melville's Writing for Readers

[Alfred Kazin was a noted critic and cultural historian. He wrote *On Native Grounds* and *The Inmost Leaf*, among his vast volume of work. In this criticism, he explains how Herman Melville wrote *Moby-Dick* for his readers.]

Moby-Dick is not only a very big book; it is also a peculiarly full and rich one, and from the very opening it conveys a sense of abundance, of high creative power, that exhilarates and enlarges the imagination. This quality is felt immediately in the style, which is remarkably easy, natural and "American," yet always literary, and which swells in power until it takes on some of the roaring and uncontainable rhythms with which Melville audibly describes the sea. The best description of this style is Melville's own, when he speaks of the "bold and nervous lofty language" that Nantucket whaling captains learn straight from nature. We feel this abundance in heroic types like the Nantucketers themselves, many of whom are significantly named after Old Testament prophets and kings, for these, too, are mighty men, and the mightiest of them all, Captain Ahab, will challenge the very order of the creation itself. This is the very heart of the book—so much so that we come to feel that there is some shattering magnitude of theme before Melville as he writes, that as a writer he had been called to an heroic new destiny.

It is this constant sense of power that constitutes the book's appeal to us, that explains its hold on our attention. *Moby-Dick* is one of those books that try to bring in as much of life as a writer can get both hands on. Melville even tries to create an image of life itself as a ceaseless creation. The book is written with a personal force of style, a passionate learning, a steady insight into our forgotten connections with the primitive. It sweeps everything before it; it gives us the happiness that only great vigor inspires.

If we start by opening ourselves to this abundance and force, by welcoming not merely the story itself, but the manner in which it speaks to us, we shall recognize in this restlessness, this richness, this persistent atmosphere of magnitude, the essential image on which the book is founded. For *Moby-Dick* is not so much a book *about* Captain Ahab's quest for the whale as it is an experience of that quest. This is only to say, what we say of any true poem, that we cannot reduce its essential substance to a subject, that we should not intellectualize and summarize it, but that we should recognize that its very force and beauty lie in the way it is conceived and written, in the qualities that flow from its being a unique entity.

In these terms, *Moby-Dick* seems to be far more of a poem than it is a novel, and since it is a narrative, to be an epic, a long poem on an heroic theme, rather than the kind of realistic fiction that we know today. Of course Melville did not deliberately set out to write a formal epic; but half-consciously, he drew upon many of the traditional characteristics of epic in order to realize the utterly original kind of novel *he* needed to write in his time—the spaciousness of theme and subject, the martial atmosphere, the association of these homely and savage materials with universal myths, the symbolic wanderings of the hero, the indispensable strength of such a hero in Captain Ahab. Yet beyond all this, what distinguishes *Moby-Dick* from modern prose fiction, what ties it up with the older, more formal kind of narrative that was once written in verse, is the fact that Melville is not interested in the meanness, the literal truthfulness, the representative slice of life, that we think of as the essence of modern realism. His book has the true poetic emphasis in that the whole story is constantly being meditated and unravelled through a single mind. (...)

Yet utterly alone as he is at the end of the book, floating on the Pacific Ocean, he manages, buoyed up on a coffin that magically serves as his life-buoy, to give us the impression that life itself can be honestly confronted only in the loneliness of each human heart.

—Alfred Kazin, "'Introduction' to *Moby-Dick*." *Melville: A Collection of Critical Essays*, ed. Richard Chase (Englewood Cliffs: Prentice Hall, Inc., 1962).

Richard Chase on Spinning Facts into Fiction

[Richard Chase was an educator and a critic. He was a Professor at Columbia University, and has written *Herman Melville*, *Walt Whitman Reconsidered*, *The American Novel and Its Tradition* and *The Democratic Vista*. In this essay he shows us how Melville took a factual story and created the novel Moby-Dick.]

What caused this flowering of Melville's genius cannot, of course, be known. But figuring prominently in the miracle must be his rereading of Shakespeare during the time he was working on the book. The influence of *Lear* and *Macbeth* is felt as one beholds Ahab and listens to his speeches and soliloquies. The language and metaphor of Shakespeare make themselves strongly felt in *Moby-Dick*, though not, we observe, in the earlier chapters. Probably it occurred to Melville, as he paused in the process of writing, that two factual narratives about whaling which he had read might be woven into his narrative—one concerning the ramming and sinking by a whale of the Nantucket ship *Essex*, another concerning a monstrous white whale called "Mocha Dick." It is probable too that he discovered that the legends, tall tales, and folklore of whaling could be more than embellishments to his narrative; they could be for him what other bodies of folklore had been for Homer, Virgil, or Camoëns (an author of whom Melville was fond)—the materials of an epic. Finally, one may suppose that partly under the influence of Hawthorne he saw that Ahab might be not only a quasi-Shakespearean hero, doomed by an inordinate pride or tragic ignorance, but also the protagonist in a kind of Puritan inner drama, a drama of the mind in its isolation and obsession. For if Ahab is akin to Shakespeare's heroes, he is more so to such Hawthorne characters as Chillingworth, the pattern of whose life also became, in Hawthorne's phrase, "a dark necessity."

The reason one is interested in the process by which *Moby-Dick* evolved from a travelogue to the complex book that it is, is that as readers we often seem to share Melville's excitement as he and we make new discoveries—as we push farther into the unknown and find metaphors and formulations that make the unknown knowable. Melville thought of art as a process, as an emergent, ever creative, but never completed metaphor. Thus he makes his imaginary poet in *Mardi* triumphantly exclaim, in reference to the epic he has written, "I have created the creative!" In taking the view that a work of art is not a completed object but is an imperfect form which should be left only potentially complete, Melville is much closer to Whitman than to Hawthorne. And what he says about the technical whaling sections of *Moby-Dick* applies as well to the whole book.

> It was stated at the outset, that this system would not be here, and at once, perfected. You cannot but plainly see that I have kept my word. But I now leave my Cetological System standing thus unfinished, even as the great Cathedral of Cologne was left, with the crane still standing upon the top of the uncompleted tower. For small erections may be finished by their first architects; grand ones, true ones, ever leave the copestone to posterity. God keep me from ever completing anything. This whole book is but a draught—nay, but the draught of a draught. Oh, Time, Strength, Cash, and Patience!

Moby-Dick, like the cathedral with the crane on its tower, allows us to see—in fact insists that we shall see—some of the machinery by which it was built, some of the processes of construction. Two passages may be quoted in this connection. The first was presumably interpolated in Chapter 16 and sounds, as Mr. Stewart suggests, like something one might as soon expect to find in a novelist's notebook as in his novel. Melville seems almost to be arguing himself into believing that a tragic hero might be made out of a Nantucket whaleman, especially if he spoke in the Quaker manner:

> So that there are instances among [the Nantucketers] of men, who, named with Scripture names—a singularly common fashion on the island—and in childhood naturally imbibing the stately dramatic thee and thou of the Quaker idiom; still, from the audacious, daring, and boundless adventure of their subsequent lives, strangely blend with these unoutgrown peculiarities, a thousand bold dashes of character, not unworthy of a Scandinavian sea-king, or a poetical Pagan

Roman. And when these things unite in a man of greatly superior natural force, with a globular brain and a ponderous heart; who has also by the stillness and seclusion of many long night-watches in the remotest waters, and beneath constellations never seen here at the north, been led to think untraditionally and independently; receiving all nature's sweet or savage impressions fresh from her own virgin voluntary and confiding breast, and thereby chiefly, but with some help from accidental advantages, to learn a bold and nervous lofty language—that man makes one in a whole nation's census—a mighty pageant creature, formed for noble tragedies. Nor will it at all detract from him, dramatically regarded, if either by birth or other circumstances, he have what seems a half wilful overruling morbidness at the bottom of his nature. For all men tragically great are made so through a certain morbidness. Be sure of this, O young ambition, all mortal greatness is but disease.

In this passage we join in the discovery of ideas that were to produce Ahab. In Chapter 14, "Nantucket," we participate in the process by which an epic emerges—namely, by the transmutation of the central facts about the life of a culture into poetry by means of the accretion of folklore, legend, and myth. The wavelike amplification and building-up, followed by the lyric subsidence at the end, is characteristic of Melville's imagination and is similar to the action of the book as a whole, as well as to various sections of it.

—Richard Chase, "Melville and *Moby-Dick*." *Melville: A Collection of Critical Essays*, ed. Richard Chase (Englewood Cliffs: Prentice Hall, Inc., 1962).

Paul Brodtkorb, Jr. on Ishmael as Storyteller

[Paul Brodtkorb, Jr. is Associate Professor Emeritus at Hunter College. In addition to *Ishmael's White World*, he has written essays on Melville's *The Confidence Man*, *Billy Budd* and Hawthorne's *The Marble Fan*.]

"Call me Ishmael," we are told. But that name is equivocally stated, despite the abruptly imperative form of its declaration. The narrator precisely does *not* say that his name *is* Ishmael; or even that he is called Ishmael as a kind of nickname. "Call me Ishmael," he says, and immediately the diction of affable informality followed by the shock of the biblical name which is both formal and highly unlikely puts us in the presence of someone who for reasons of his own would rather not say who he really is.

If "Ishmael" is self-adopted, it is, with all its allusiveness, doubtless a more accurate designation of him than its sayer's real name, for it clearly signifies his sense of himself and his world. But because behind the show of affability a real name is withheld, Ishmael remains to some extent a stranger, and a man in a false position; and because he does, as soon as the self-bestowed name is spoken, the shadow of nothingness is upon the book.

That shadow lengthens when we note the contradictory details that slips of memory betray the narrator into. The playful but ultimately serious hyperbole, intended to win us over; the authoritative reporting of unknowable or imaginary events; the fanciful ties, such as the Town-Ho's story—these darken the shadow. "Ishmael," we soon discover, is a storyteller in every sense; he tells us a fish story that, like most fish stories, is partly true and partly false.

Yet he is not especially anxious to conceal this from us. On the contrary, "storyteller" is the first and continuing guise in which he presents himself. At times he explicitly discusses the problems of a storyteller in creating atmosphere and plausibility. At other times he shows himself manipulating the truth:

> "Do tell, now," cried, Bildad, "is this Philistine a regular member of Deacon Deuteronomy's meeting? I never saw him going there, and I pass it every Lord's day."
>
> "I don't know anything about Deacon Deuteronomy or his meeting," said I, "all I know is, that Queequeg here is a born member of the First Congregational Church. He is a deacon himself, Queequeg is."
>
> "Young man," said Bildad sternly, "thou art skylarking with me—explain thyself, thou young Hittite. What church dost thee mean? answer me."
>
> Finding myself thus hard pushed, I replied.... (xviii)

Caught out in a lie, Ishmael eludes Bildad's wrath by enthusiastic embroidery of his story's loose ends. In content and circumstances, the incident is typical of Ishmael's lies, the facts of which if based on actuality are already highly interpreted by self-interested exegesis. More important, however, is what this sort of incident—the Town-Ho's story, though a more disinterested, virtuoso lie, is similar in this respect—suggests about the audience of an Ishmaelean lie: Ishmael lies to those who invite his mockery. He lies to the earnest ones of the earth: the owners, aristocrats, and authorities; the stern, the righteous, or the self-satisfied; all who because of the pompous security they command are gullible. He lies, in short, to the Bildads who in being false comforters take false comfort. He lies because he strongly suspects either that their truths are lies also; or that they use their truths like lies, for their own ends.

Similarly, Ishmael lies to us: the comfortable readers of adventure stories like *Typee*, *Omoo*, and *Moby Dick*, who kill our boredom by distorting what boredom means. We are all in false positions, his attitude seems to say; and it says this at the same time that it says that his false position, because it is consciously chosen in full awareness of the alternatives, is more responsible and therefore, perversely, truer than the received and unexamined false positions of others; and in this attitude we may understand a major basis of Ishmael's respect for Ahab, whose defiant despair creates a personal truth so passionately thought-out and passionately willed that often reality crucially seems to conform to it. Like Kierkegaard, Ishmael is despairingly left with the idea that for man, in many complicated ways, subjectivity is truth; or, rather, the only truth is in subjectivity.

One result of all this is that for the pragmatic reader the prevalence of Ishmaelean lies, once recognized, must permeate with nonbeing everything that Ishmael says. Because anything is potentially untrue, the single and final reality of the events of the *Pequod*'s last voyage is to be found in Ishmael's not wholly trustworthy mind. For such a reader, *Moby Dick*'s foundations in the actuality that Ishmael pretends to report are very shaky ones: he can never lose his awareness that he is reading a novel, not something solid like the history or biography that Captain Veres prefers; moreover, he is reading a peculiarly self-subverting novel that pretends to be true (but clearly isn't) autobiography, which in turn disconcertingly combines features of epic, romance, and Menippean satire. Nowhere is there dry land. Nothing can be trusted to be what it seems, and the reader, if only for self-preservation, must have "doubts of all things earthly" (LXXXV). In a curious way, the reader is forced even against his will to share Ishmaelean attitudes.

—Paul Brodtkorb, Jr., *Ishmael's White World* by Yale University Press, 1965).

Charles Olson on Exploring Seas and America's West

[Charles Olson is a poet known for his Maximus Poems. In this work, he compares whalers on the sea to American Pioneers heading west.]

I take SPACE to be the central fact to man born in America, from Folsom cave to now. I spell it large because it comes large here. Large, and without mercy.

It is geography at bottom, a hell of wide land from the beginning. That made the first American story (Parkman's): exploration.

Something else than a stretch of earth—seas on both sides, no barriers to contain as restless a thing as Western man was becoming in Columbus' day. That made Melville's story (part of it).

PLUS a harshness we still perpetuate, a sun like a tomahawk, small earthquakes but big tornadoes and hurrikans, a river north and south in the middle of the land running out the blood.

The fulcrum of America is the Plains, half sea half land, a high sun as metal and obdurate as the iron horizon, and a man's job to square the circle.

Some men ride on such space, others have to fasten themselves like a tent stake to survive. As I see it Poe dug in and Melville mounted. They are the alternatives.

Americans still fancy themselves such democrats. But their triumphs are of the machine. It is the only master of space the average person ever knows, oxwheel to piston, muscle to jet. It gives trajectory.

To Melville it was not the will to be free but the will to overwhelm nature that lies at the bottom of us as individuals and a people. Ahab is no democrat. Moby-Dick, antagonist, is only king of natural force, resource.

I am interested in a Melville who decided sometime in 1850 to write a book about the whaling industry and what happened to a man in command of one of the most successful machines Americans had perfected up to that time—the whaleship.

This captain, Ahab by name, knew space. He rode it across seven seas. He was an able skipper, what the fishing people I was raised with call a highliner. Big catches: he brought back holds barrel full of the oil of the sperm, the light of American and European communities up to the middle of the 19th century.

This Ahab had gone wild. The object of his attention was something unconscionably big and white. He had become a specialist: he had all space concentrated into the form of a whale called Moby-Dick. And he assailed it as Columbus an ocean, LaSalle a continent, the Donner Party their winter Pass.

I am interested in a Melville who was long-eyed enough to understand the Pacific as part of our geography, another West, prefigured in the Plains, antithetical.

The beginning of man was salt sea, and the perpetual reverberation of that great ancient fact, constantly renewed in the unfolding of life in every human individual, is the important single fact about Melville. Pelagic.

He had the tradition in him, deep, in his brain, his words, the salt beat of his blood. He had the sea of himself in a vigorous, stricken way, as Poe the street. It enabled him to draw up from Shakespeare. It made Noah, and Moses, contemporary to him. History was ritual and repetition when Melville's imagination was at its own proper beat.

It was an older sense than the European man's, more to do with magic than culture. Magic which, in contrast to worship, is all black. For magic has one purpose: compel men or non-human forces to do one's will. Like Ahab, American, one aim: lordship over nature.

I am willing to ride Melville's image of man, whale and ocean to find in him prophecies, lessons he himself would not have spelled out. A hundred years gives us an advantage. For Melville was as much larger than himself as Ahab's hate. He was a plunger. He knew how to take a chance.

The man made a mess of things. He got all balled up with Christ. He made a white marriage. He had one son die of tuberculosis, the other shoot himself. He only rode his own space once—*Moby-Dick*. He had to be wild or he was nothing in particular. He had to go fast, like an American, or he was all torpor. Half horse half alligator.

Melville took an awful licking. He was bound to. He was an original, aboriginal. A beginner. It happens that way to the dreaming men it takes to discover America: Columbus and LaSalle won, and then lost her to the competent. Daniel Boone loved her earth. Harrod tells the story of coming upon Boone one day far to the west in Kentucky of where Harrod thought any white man had ever been. He heard sound he couldn't place, crept forward to a boulder and there in a blue grass clearing was Boone alone singing to himself. Boone died west of the Mississippi, in his own country criminal—"wanted," a bankrupt of spirit and land.

Beginner—and interested in beginnings. Melville had a way of reaching back through time until he got history pushed back so far he turned time into space. He was like a migrant backtrailing to Asia, some Inca trying to find a lost home.

We are the last "first" people. We forget that. We act big, misuse our land, ourselves. We lose our own primary.

Melville went back, to discover us, to come forward. He got as far as *Moby-Dick*.

—Charles Olson, "Call Me Ishmael." Originally published in *Call Me Ishmael* (City Lights Books, 1947.)

P. Adams Sitney on Ahab's Shakespearean Speech

[P. Adams Sitney teaches film and visual arts at Princeton University. In this essay, Sitney compares Captain Ahab's tone and character to some of Shakespeare's greatest works.]

In "The Symphony," the one hundred and thirty-second chapter of *Moby Dick*, the captain's dialogue with his first mate, Starbuck, drifts into a soliloquy in which he questions his control over his acts:

> What is it, what nameless, inscrutable, unearthly thing is it; what cozening, hidden lord and master, and cruel remorseless emperor commands me; that against all natural lovings and longings, I so keep pushing, and crowding and jamming myself on all the time; recklessly making me ready to do what in my own proper, natural heart, I durst not so much as dare? Is Ahab, Ahab? Is it I, God or who, that lifts this arm? But if the great sun move not of himself; but is as an errant-boy in heaven; nor one single star can revolve, but by some invisible power; how can this one small heart beat; this one small brain think thoughts; unless God does that beating, does that thinking, does that living, and not I.

In this context the tiny sentence "Is Ahab, Ahab?" appears innocent enough. The force of fate makes the captain doubt his identity. For years I read this question ignoring the comma, supporting myself with the commonplace of editors that Melville was an ungrammatical punctuator, as if the sentence were the interrogative form of the tautology: Ahab is Ahab. But what might the question "Is Ahab Ahab?" or "Is X X?" when X stands for a proper noun, mean? In the form of a question doubt is raised about the language of the tautology. It asks if there is not something wrong with the naming of X that represents X as ontologically unstable. Then again, it could be a question about two different meanings of the proper noun. Does the first X correspond fully to the stable meaning of X represented by the second instance of the name? All three readings of the question are relevant to our interpretation of *Moby Dick* as a whole: they correspond to ontological, epistemological, and typological investigations.

I would like to consider the alternatives posed by the problematic comma. If we read the second naming of Ahab as vocative, two interpretations of the sentence are possible. Either "Is Ahab...?" questions his existence, or the sentence is incomplete, requiring reference to the previous one. In that case it asks if "Ahab" is the answer to the previous question; is "Ahab" the "nameless ... thing" that "commands me." In fact, the first English edition of *The Whale*, printed months earlier than the American, explicitly determines this reading. "Is it Ahab, Ahab?" in the English text makes very good sense; for it fits all three opening sentences in this speech into a single form: "What is it... Is it Ahab ... Is it I, God, or who...."

We cannot conclude whether this is one of the many editorial intrusions to be found in *The Whale* or a genuine alternative from Melville's hand. Let's consider the consequences of accepting it as the superior reading. The ontological question posed by both "Is Ahab Ahab?" and "Is Ahab ... ?" disappears. Nevertheless, the repetition of the name in the vocative continues to underscore the potential ambiguity of the name which has both epistemological and typological consequences. It is this doubling of the name, consistent in both texts, which I take to be crucial; for it points up the relationship of the name to the dilemmas of identity and responsibility. Therefore, even though I prefer the richer ambiguities of the American version, what follows will not depend upon the choice of texts.

My conviction that "Is Ahab, Ahab?" should be read as the questioning of a tautology rests on the echoing passage two chapters later in "The Chase—Second Day" when the captain refers back to his earlier encounter with the first mate:

> Starbuck, of late I've felt strangely moved to thee; ever since that hour we both saw—thou know'st what, in one another's eyes. But in this matter of the whale, be thy face to me as the palm of this hand—a lipless, unfeatured blank. Ahab is for ever Ahab, man. This whole act's immutably decreed. 'Twas rehearsed by thee and me a billion years before this ocean rolled. Fool! I am the Fates' lieutenant; I act under orders.

"Ahab is for ever Ahab, man" reasserts the ontological question of the earlier chapter in the rhetoric of bravado, taking the tautology out of the realm of time which had oppressed the captain, who feared that Moby Dick would be taken by a rival whaler or that he would not live to do the job. Now that he is in the midst of the "fiery hunt," he speaks as though he were reconciled to his relationship to Fate. But readers soon discover that he is haunted during this speech by hints of the fulfillment of Fedallah's prophecy of his death.

The paired lines "Is Ahab, Ahab!" and "Ahab is for ever Ahab" do not dispell the ambiguities we found in the name, Ahab. The later speech proclaims that Ahab is an ontological entity, that his name is appropriate, and that he conforms to the model of the ancient, Biblical Ahab.

The tone of these speeches is familiar enough. Melville wrote fresh from a reading of Shakespeare. The use of the name, instead of "I," in the mouth of the hero recalls a number of precedents in the plays:

> ... O Lear, Lear, Lear!
> Beat at this gate, that let thy folly in
> And thy dear judgment out!
> (*King Lear*, Act I, sc. iv.)

> Was't Hamlet wronged Laertes? Never Hamlet.
> If Hamlet from himself be ta'en away,
> And when he's not himself does wrong Laertes,
> Then Hamlet does it not, Hamlet denies it.
> Who does it then? His madness. If it'd be so,
> Hamlet is of the faction that is wronged,
> His madness is poor Hamlet's enemy.
> (*Hamlet*, Act V, sc. ii.)

Shakespeare uses this substitution of the third for the first person, of the name for I, here in parallel speeches by Othello, Brutus, and Timon, to emphasize the machinations of fate or to dramatize the dislocation of selfhood in madness. Its illusion of objectivity indicates that the speaker has submitted to the language and the judgment of the world by renouncing his power to speak for himself. To make such a renunciation is to invoke the discourse of the victim.

Melville became excessively fond of this mode of self-address. It is a mark of Ahab's grandiosity. Interpreting the Ecuadorian doubloon he nailed to the mast as a reward for the first sighting of Moby Dick, he repeats his name four times: "The firm tower, that is Ahab; the volcano, that is Ahab; the courageous, undaunted, and victorious fowl, that, too, is Ahab; all are Ahab;

and this round gold is but the image of the rounder globe, which, like a magician's glass, to each and every man in turn but mirrors back its own mysterious self." As much echo as mirror, the coin reflects his name again and again.

In *Moby Dick* calling oneself by name is not Ahab's exclusive privilege. Stubb does it with comic effect when he finds himself unfairly treated by the captain. The narrator calls himself by his pseudonym three times in "A Bower in the Arsacides," as if, taking the side of his readers, he felt the need to demand evidence of his authority for the whale lore he was about to expound. These whimsical versions of the discourse of victimization are not of the same order of frequency or dramatic intensity as Ahab's use of his own name. He embraces and sublimates his victimization, naming himself as if being called Ahab were an honor and a responsibility of which he was proud.

—P. Adams Sitney, "Ahab's Name: A Reading of the Symphony." *Modern Critical Views: Herman Melville*, ed. Harold Bloom (New York: Chelsea House Publishers, 1986).

Neal L. Tolchin on Melville's Mourning

[Neal L. Tolchin is a Professor in the English department at Hunter College. He has also written articles on Melville's *Redburn*. In this essay he looks at *Moby-Dick* as Melville's way of mourning. The characters' grief comes from events in the author's life.]

Deep & Secret grief is a cannibal of its own heart.
—Bacon

Deep memories yield no epitaphs
—Herman Melville, *Moby-Dick*

Two gender-related findings of the Harvard Study of Bereavement illuminate the role of mourning in *Moby-Dick*. (...) the male subjects of this study tend to define their sense of loss in terms of dismemberment, whereas the women studied register a sense of abandonment. The preceding chapters of this book have demonstrated that the imagery of dismemberment pervades Melville's work. Ahab's dismasted state, however, most dramatically performs this social symbolization of male bereavement. The Harvard Study has also found that one-third of the women interviewed displayed "generalized hostility" three weeks after their loss, while none of the men showed this reaction. Nevertheless, the male subjects reported that it took them longer to feel that they had overcome their bereavement; a third of the men reported an inability to cry, claiming that they felt choked up.[1] And it is this finding that takes us deeply into the complexities of grief and gender in *Moby-Dick*.

In his shattered sense of corporeal and psychic wholeness, Ahab is Melville's most uninhibited male mourner. The rage that surfaces in Ahab's character contrasts starkly with the genteel denial of anger often exhibited by Melville's male characters—the important exception to this being Ahab's prototype, *Redburn*'s Jackson. Contemporaries of Melville could simply not accept the extent to which Ahab melodramatically vents his morbidity: this was the object of sharp attacks on the novel. Twentieth-century critics turn Ahab into anything but what Melville portrayed him as: a bereaved monomaniac. Ahab still expresses dark feelings which Melville's readers feel more comfortable translating into less painful abstractions.[2]

Why does Melville allow Ahab a heightened bereavement? Elsewhere in his fiction he largely obeys the cultural codes that burden women with the public symbolization of grief. I contend that Ahab performs the social role ascribed to the female mourner—although he exceeds even that role in the intensity of his public expression of grief—because his character is shaped by Melville's sense of his mother's conflicted grief for his father. Through Ahab's character, Melville portrays the power of his mother's bereaved rage and its crucial influence on his own grief for his father. Although Ahab's identification with Maria Melville's grief is kept on the novel's margins, it momentarily breaches the surface in "The Candles," where Ahab, while attempting to "'read my sire,'" claims for himself a "'queenly personality.'" Ishmael portrays Ahab as both the damned maniac and the embattled hero in quest of an ultimate showdown with all the Evil in the universe, but Ahab's divided delineation has a great deal to do with the contradictory images of Maria's husband, as damned deathbed maniac and as an idealized figure that she communicated to her son through her conflicted grief.[3]

Ahab represents Melville's attempt to exorcise from his inner world the complex image of his father he internalized from his mother's grief. For this reason, Ahab exhibits the symptoms of Allan Melvill's last weeks of life: deathbed mania. Through Crazy Ahab, Melville attempts to transform the mania into both penetrating insight into the tragic dimensions of existence and the heroic resistance to Fixed Fate. Ahab's characterization expresses a doubleness that goes to the heart of the energies of the novel. A morbid figure and one of tragic grandeur, his character opens itself both to Melville's fears of the paternal image of the deathbed maniac that threatened him from within and to Melville's sense of the overwhelming and dangerous rage of his own unresolved grief, compounded by the influence of the rage of a mother's grief on the anger of a child's sense of abandonment by his parent.[4]

Ahab exists as the object of perception and creation of Ishmael, a narrator marked especially by a mordant sense of humor and by occasional insights into the complexity and the fluidity of reality underlying social representations. However, Ishmael's narration also often participates in the Victorian American social codes that militate against the public expression of intense feeling, such as what his culture termed excessive grief.[5] And both Ahab and Ishmael share the stage with a "tremendous apparition," Moby Dick (448). While, on the one hand, Ishmael perceives that the whale "must remain unpainted to the last"—"I have ever found your plain things the knottiest of all," he observes slyly—on the other hand, Ishmael views Ahab's intense bereavement through the cultural codes that cause Ahab to harbor "the mad secret of his unabated rage bolted up and keyed in him" while he endeavors to appear "but naturally grieved" after his return from the voyage on which Moby Dick sheared off his leg (228, 312, 162, 161). By portraying Ahab's unnatural bereavement in terms of his culture's social construction of grief and madness, Ishmael dramatizes how he must view Ahab's excessive grief in terms of monomania.

As Ishmael oscillates between his mixed response to Ahab's grief—he both condemns Ahab for expressing intense bereavement and enviously idealizes him for doing so—and Moby Dick's resistance to representation, the novel generates much of the energy and excitement of its rich language. This narrative shifting, combined with Ishmael's penchant for shiftiness as a narrator, splits Melville's attempt to represent his unresolved grief into confrontation with an incarnation of his living linking object role and his respect for the complexity of feeling that eludes social representations. When Moby Dick finally appears, Ishmael's imagery intimates his sense of the whale as "a thing writ in water," an inscription of the natural world's fluid writing but also an echo of Keats's gravestone epitaph: "Here lies one whose name was writ in water" (453).[6]

Both grief and the white whale, the novel suggests, cannot finally be possessed in the terms of social representation available to Ishmael. The theme of possession comes to the fore when Ishmael angrily protests against the legal argument that assumes women are property. "Possession," in Ishmael's scathing analysis, has become "the whole of the law" (333). In his representation of Moby Dick, which obliquely critiques his own convention-bound portrayal of Ahab's intense bereavement, Ishmael attempts to subvert patriarchal social codes in his preference for a more fluid state of affairs, one in which his readers are "but a Loose-Fish and a Fast-Fish, too" (334). The "'fluid consciousness'" Sophia Hawthorne perceived in Melville transforms *Moby-Dick*'s readers into Fast-Fish, held by a Loose-Fish of complex narrative animation—one that seduces us into the powerful experience of morbid grief, which threatens to subvert from within the melodramatic generic languages in which Ahab comes to life.[7]

NOTES

1. Melville cites the "Deep and Secret grief" quote from Bacon in notes, probably made in the summer of 1849, on the flyleaf of vol. 7 of his edition of Shakespeare, which contained *Lear*, *Othello*, and *Hamlet*. Charles Olson reproduces only part of these notes (*Call Me Ishmael* [San Francisco: City Lights Books, 1947], 39, 52). For the Bacon quote see Luther Mansfield and Howard P. Vincent, eds., *Moby-Dick* (New York: Hendricks House, 1952), 643–44. In their invaluable notes, they also cite De Quincey, whom Melville read shortly before he began *Moby-Dick*, on the "mysterious handwritings of grief" in the brain, which "are not dead, but sleeping.... In some potent convulsion of the system, all wheels back into its earliest elemental stage" (704). On the Harvard study, see Ira Glick et al., *The First Year of Bereavement* (New York: John Wiley and Sons, 1974), chap. 13, 261–82, esp. 263–65, 271.

2. On antebellum reviewers' detestation of what they called "morbidity," see Nina Baym, *Novels, Readers, and Reviewers: Responses to Fiction in Antebellum America* (Ithaca: Cornell University Press, 1984), 142. For instance, *House of Seven Gables* was found "morbid" by one reviewer (Baym, *Novels, Readers, and Reviewers*, 177). Melville seems to be playing on this popular prejudice when he identifies Ahab as poisoned by "'a half-wilful overruling morbidness at the bottom of his nature'" (*Moby-Dick*, eds. Harrison Hayford and Hershel Parker [New York: Norton, 1967], 111; hereafter cited in the text). Melville's crony, Evert Duyckinck, mockingly objects to *Moby-Dick*'s "association of whaling and lamentation," which seemed to him "why blubber is popularly associated with tears." *Southern Quarterly Review* (Jan. 1852) calls Ahab "a monstrous bore"; and the *London Morning Advertiser* (Oct. 24, 1851) complains of Ahab's madness: "'Somewhat too much of this!'" (in Mansfield and Vincent, eds., *Moby-Dick*, xvii, xx; and Watson G. Branch, *Melville: The Critical Heritage* [London: Routledge and Kegan Paul, 1974], 252).

For an exploration of monomania in Melville's culture, see Henry Nash Smith, *Democracy and the Novel* (New York: Oxford University Press, 1978), chap. 3, 35–55; and Vieda Skultans, *Madness and Morals: Ideas on Insanity in the Nineteenth Century* (London: Routledge and Kegan, Paul, 1975).

See Mansfield and Vincent's introduction for a good survey of attitudes of early twentieth-century critics to Ahab. After the 1920s, when critics identified Ahab with Melville, the tendency was to identify Ahab with the various bogeymen of the critic's political moment. However, such critics as William Ellery Sedgwick (1944) could speak of "Ahab's noble madness that sprang from an excess of humanity" (Mansfield and Vincent, eds., *Moby-Dick*, xxvii).

3. Mansfield and Vincent note that the aspect of the biblical Ahab's story which most interested Melville's contemporaries was Ahab's usurpation of Naboth's paternal inheritance, his vineyard (*Moby-Dick*, n. to 637). Melville might have been unconsciously drawn to Ahab in part by the way this appropriation mirrored how his mother's bereaved image of his father displaced his own sense of paternal identification and inheritance. For the way Ahab's story was used in antebellum political rhetoric, see Michael Paul Rogin, *Subversive Genealogy: The Politics and Art of Herman Melville* (New York: Knopf, 1983), chap. 4, 102–54. Rogin gives a fine precis of the earlier political readings and he goes beyond them by transforming the political allegories of these critics into a sense for how *Moby-Dick*'s language is "deeply enmeshed in the crisis of 1850," i.e., the slavery issue in the U.S. and the failed revolutions abroad (*Subversive Genealogy*, 107). Rogin draws attention especially to how "Melville's family connections to Indian dispossession and slavery" left their mark on his art (*Subversive Genealogy*, 107, 143). The scholarship Rogin summarizes includes William T. Weathers, "*Moby-Dick* and the Nineteenth-Century Scene," *Texas Studies in Literature and Language* 1 (Winter 1960): 477–501; Charles H. Foster, "Something in Emblems: A Reinterpretation of *Moby-Dick*," *The New England Quarterly* 34 (Mar. 1961): 3–35; and Alan Heimert. "*Moby-Dick* and American Political Symbolism," *American Quarterly* 16 (Apr. 1963): 498–534.

In the source that Mansfield and Vincent suggest for Fedallah—*1001 Days, Persian Tales*—a dervish, who possesses the power of "'reanimating a dead body, by flinging my own Soul into it,'" revives a dead nightingale to assuage a queen's grief (*Moby-Dick*, 732). For a different view of Ahab's claim to a "queenly personality," see Robert Zoellner: "This is superb rhetoric, but it is false fact. Ahab has willfully destroyed his 'personality,' and obliterated its 'queenly' freedom" (*The Salt-Sea Mastodon: A Reading of* Moby-Dick [Berkeley: University of California Press, 1973], 100).

T. Walker Herbert argues that in his grief for his father Melville simultaneously absolved him and identified with his mother's probable damnation of him from her Dutch Reformed perspective. Allan's death shattered a tenuous balance in which Melville had been able to harmonize his parents' respective Unitarian and Dutch Reformed views. See Chap. 1 for my reading of Maria's idiosyncratic Calvinism, one more mixed with genteel codes than Herbert implies (*Moby-Dick and Calvinism: A World Dismantled* [New Brunswick, N.J.: Rutgers University Press, 1977], chap. 3, 57–68, esp. 60–61).

As noted in Chapter 1, given that Allan Melvill appeared in her life shortly after her heroic father, General Peter Gansevoort, died, Maria may have turned Allan into a living linking object to her father. If so, this may illuminate Ishmael's need to imbue Ahab with excessive heroic qualities, at the same time that Ahab's damnation suggests that he is being viewed from Maria's Dutch Reformed perspective.

Nathalia Wright points out that the biblical Ahab is already a figure of doubleness: he is a composite of two sources, one of which found him able and the other viewed him as a dangerous innovator (*Melville's Use of the Bible* [Durham, N.C.: Duke University Press, 1949]. 62).

4. Putting the stress on the cultural context of what he finds to be Melville's religious crisis, Herbert argues that by allowing "spiritual dislocations" and their attendant "feverish excitement" to surface, Melville "became convinced that his true creativeness lay in braving this tumult, winning the articulation of a 'vital truth,' in contention with apparent madness." Herbert links Ahab to Allan insofar as both could be described as liberal heretics as depicted by Calvinist rhetoric (*Moby-Dick and Calvinism*, 18, 40).

Richard Chase reads Ahab as "both father and son" (cited in Mansfield and Vincent, eds., *Moby-Dick*, xxix). Newton Arvin characterizes Moby Dick as an "archetypal Parent ... the mother also, so far as she becomes a substitute for the father." Moby Dick also evokes "the violently contradictory emotions that prevail between parent and child" (*Herman Melville* [New York: William Sloane, 1950], 173). Edwin Haviland Miller calls *Moby-Dick* "a study of the rivalry of the 'son' (Ishmael) with the father (Ahab)"; and he finds that "Ahab fathers Ishmael," in as much as the latter writes the former's story (*Herman Melville: A Biography* [New York: Braziller, 1975], 182, 210).

5. See Francis Parkman, "Occasions and Remedy of Excessive Grief," in *An Offering of Sympathy to the Afflicted* ... 3d ed. (Boston: James Monroe & Co., 1842), 109–17. Baym argues that antebellum reviewers viewed the novel as "an agent of social control" (*Novels, Readers, and Reviewers*, 170). One contemporary reviewer, conflating Ishmael and Melville, describes the novel's narrator as performing with "the ease and polish of a finished gentleman" (*Philadelphia American Saturday Courier* [Nov. 22, 1851], cited in Hershel Parker and Harrison Hayford, eds., *Moby-Dick as Doubloon: Essays and Extracts 1851–1970* [New York: Norton, 1970], 52).

Critics rarely review Ishmael negatively. Zoellner, though, notes that the verbal resolutions which satisfy Ishmael do not satisfy Melville (*Salt-Sea Mastodon*, 216). Deploying Sacvan Bercovitch on the jeremiad, James Duban subtly argues that "the exclusive tendencies of the covenant psychology undergirding all jeremiads lead Ishmael to betray the abolitionist egalitarianisms he purports to champion." "Ishmael ... is the American child who trips over his own conceptual shoestrings while seeking to flee the brutality of his nation's past" (*Melville's Major Fiction: Politics, Theology, and Imagination* [DeKalb: Northern Illinois University Press, 1983], 108, 137).

6. Cited in David Perkins, ed., *English Romantic Writers* (New York: Harcourt Brace Jovanovich, 1967), 1115. See Mansfield and Vincent, eds., *Moby-Dick*, 827. They also suggest that the biblical Moab, a possible source for *Moby*, in Hebrew means "seed of the father," while *Ahab* in Hebrew means "the brother of the father," or "uncle or father of the brother" (*Moby-Dick*, 695, 637). This last etymology bears on Edward Edinger's suggestion that Maria did not commit herself emotionally to her husband but remained attached to her family, esp. her brother: "making the psychic atmosphere of Melville's family that of a matriarchy in which the mother is the central figure and the masculine authority resides not with the father but with the maternal uncle" (*Melville's* Moby-Dick: *A Jungian Commentary: An American Nekyia* [New York: New Directions, 1975], 7–8). In his letters, Allan addresses Peter Gansevoort as brother.

7. Sophia Hawthorne cited in Eleanor Melville Metcalf, *Herman Melville: Cycle and Epicycle* (Cambridge: Harvard University Press, 1953), 106.

—Neal L. Tolchin, "A Thing Writ in Water: Allan Melville's Epitaph," *Mourning, Gender, and Creativity in the Art of Herman Melville.* (Yale University Press, 1988).

Leo Bersani on Homosexual Relationships

[Leo Bersani is a Professor of French at the University of California at Berkley. He has written *Marcel Proust: The Fictions of Life and Art*, *A Future for Astyanax: Character and Desire in Literature*, *The Freudian Body: Psychoanalysis and Art*. In this work, he explores the evidence of Homosexuality in *Moby-Dick*.]

Much has been made of homoeroticism in *Moby-Dick*, and this is not astonishing in view of the novel's hints in this direction.[6] The major piece of presumed evidence is of course the Ishmael–Queequeg relation, in which Ishmael seems not at all reluctant to portray himself as the huge savage's contented wife. On the one hand, as a couple Ishmael and Queequeg both prefigure and personalize the fraternal feelings in such tasks as cutting into the whale's blubber and reconverting its sperm into liquid. On the other hand, Ishmael gives a highly eroticized account of the friendship. After their first night together in the same bed at the Spouter Inn in New Bedford, Ishmael awakes to find Queequeg's arm thrown over him "in the most loving and affectionate manner," as if he "had been his wife" and were being held in a "bridegroom clasp" (32–33). The next night they seal their friendship, once again in bed, with "confidential disclosures," just as man and wife often choose their bed to "open the very bottom of their souls to each other." "Thus, then," this passage ends, "in our hearts' honeymoon, lay I and Queequeg—a cosy, loving pair" (54). During the voyage, when they are both tied to the same monkey rope (in the "humorously perilous business" of Queequeg's going over the side of the ship to insert a blubber hook into the whale's back, where he must remain during the whole stripping operation), they are not simply "inseparable twin brother[s]" but are "for the time ... wedded" (271).

There is no ambiguity whatsoever in all these eroticizing allusions. They clearly instruct us to think of the bond between Ishmael and Queequeg as not unlike marital bonds, and it can be argued that they do this with no suggestion of homosexual desire. I say this somewhat tentatively because we might also say that homosexual desire is precisely what is signified by those conjugal signifiers. But where exactly is the signified? Is there a *subject* of homosexual desire in *Moby-Dick*? Far from representing either unequivocal homosexuality or surfaces of heterosexual desire troubled by repressed homosexual impulses, Melville's characters have no sexual subjectivity at all. Critics readily admit how little the wholly improbable soliloquies of Melville's characters conform to the discursive parameters of realistic fiction; they have more difficulty recognizing that those soliloquies adequately represent the essence of the characters. Interiority in *Moby-Dick* is almost entirely philosophical; each character is a certain confluence of metaphysical, epistemological, and social-ethical positions. Homoeroticism can enter the novel so easily because, psychologically, there is nothing at stake. In Balzac, Gide, and Proust, homosexual desire is a fact of great psychological significance, whereas it may be a peculiarity of American literature—Cooper, Twain, and Hemingway come to mind—that it frequently presents homosexual situations that are psychologically inconsequential, unconnected to characterization. Ishmael's marital metaphors reveal nothing about him because there is nowhere in the novel an Ishmael about whom such metaphors can be revealing.

This does not mean that they are unimportant: their very significance depends on *not* providing an intelligible alternative to Ahab's despotism. Each time the novel spells out any such alternative, it is in terms that do little more than negatively repeat what they oppose. Thus the land is opposed to the sea, and Ahab's unhappy solitude is set against the quiet joy of domestic ties. Starbuck is the principal advocate of intelligible alternatives to Ahab, such as wife and family, the land, fraternal compassion, and a democratic respect for the rights of others. But if Ahab's tyrannical rule enacts the ultimate logic of the privileges that democracy would accord personality, then perhaps the very principle of oppositional couplings cannot be trusted. Only something that does not enter into logical opposition can be "opposed" to Ahab. Politically this means that in order to escape the antidemocratic consequences inherent in the democratic ideal, a type of social relation must be imagined that is neither autocratic nor democratic.

Ishmael's response to Queequeg and the crew is the testing of this other relation, although each time he tries to analyze it he also banalizes it, as in the Starbuck-like contrast between the intellect and the fireside. But, just as Ishmael's insane ecstasy while squeezing blobs of sperm is irreducible to any of these terms, so the introduction of homoeroticism into the novel prevents his representation of Queequeg and the crew from being one of a society united in the bonds of friendship created by communal work. This homoeroticism, however, never settles into what would be merely another type of oppositional grouping. By figuring what I have called a nonpsychological homosexuality, Melville proposes a social bond based not on subordination to the great personality embodied by Ahab, not on the democratic ideal of power distributed according to intrinsic worth, not on those feelings binding either two friends or the partners in a marriage, not, finally, on the transgressed homage to all such legitimated social bonds in conventional images of homosexual desire. (Proust serves as a good example of the homosexual writer unable, for the most part, to account for his own desires except as transgressive replications of the socially accepted bonds they only superficially exclude.)

The casual humor of both the early section on Ishmael's "marriage" to Queequeg and the description of sperm squeezing helps to transform the representation of both friendship and homoeroticism into an inconceivable social bond. In so doing it evokes, in an unexpected way, the originality of American society, which Melville is both attached to and unable to describe. Ishmael's humor is a way of simultaneously proposing and withdrawing definitions and identifications, of using what are, after all, the only available categories, social and linguistic, to coax into existence as yet unavailable terms. Even the most inappropriate descriptions can serve this dislocating function. Thus, though I may have been right to argue that the reference to wife, heart, and fireside is a taming irrelevance in the squeezing-sperm chapter, the terms also disturbingly suggest an unformulated relation between a kind of anarchic sensuality and a socially viable domesticity. Similarly, far from being a parodistic version of normal marriage or a domesticating of homosexual bonds, the Ishmael–Queequeg marriage enacts a sensuality that cannot be reduced to the psychology of either heterosexual or homosexual desire, a sensuality at once nontransgressive and authorized by nothing beyond Ishmael's mode of addressing it.

Lest this begin to sound like an argument for the socially unthreatening nature of homoeroticism, I want to insist on the absence of authorization. Melville makes it clear that the society in which these new relations are being tested is a society wholly outside society. From the very first pages, going to sea is presented as a letting go of all social, conceptual, and sexual familiarity. The first chapter of *Moby-Dick* is an extraordinarily haunting invocation of seagoing as a "substitute for pistol and ball," a deliberate removal from life itself. A whole city is transformed into a collective suicidal longing when Ishmael evokes thousands of men "posted like silent sentinels all around the town" and "fixed in ocean reveries." We should keep in mind this powerfully oneiric image of a humanity thronging "just as nigh the water as they possibly can without falling in," anxious to abandon the ship of society for the magnetizing and original death promised by the sea. The first chapter clearly warns us not to consider any bonds or fellowship that may develop or, in the case of Ishmael or Queequeg, be confirmed on board the *Pequod* as compatible with the society of the land.

NOTE

6. To mention two ends of a kind of moral spectrum of perspectives on homosexuality in *Moby-Dick*: Leslie Fiedler, in *Love and Death in the American Novel* (New York: Stein and Day, 1966), finds Melville (and other American writers) unable to deal with adult heterosexual love. Robert K. Martin, in *Hero, Captain, and Stranger: Male Friendship, Social Critique, and Literary Form in the Sea Novels of Herman Melville* (Chapel Hill: University of North Carolina Press, 1986), reinterprets this failure as an accomplishment of the highest order. "The homosexual relationship," he writes, "is invested by Melville with radical social potential; it is through the affirmation of the values of nonaggressive male-bonded couples that the power of the patriarch can be contested and even defeated" (p. 70). Martin's argument has an engaging specificity. The patriarchal structure might be broken down by a kind of communal masturbatory narcissism: "Men coming together [in group masturbation] are not men fighting each other, or even men hurting whales" (p. 82). The pacification of the phallus through masturbation remains, however, a problematic notion.

—Leo Bersani, "Incomparable America," *The Culture of Redemption* (Harvard University Press, 1990).

SHAWN THOMSON ON THE OPPOSING FORCES THAT SHAPE *MOBY-DICK*

[Shawn Thomson is a Graduate Teaching Assistant at the University of Kansas, and has written *The Romantic Architecture of Herman Melville's* Moby-Dick. In this essay, Thomson examines the contradictory forces that shape *Moby-Dick*, including the opposites of Ishmael and Ahab, reality and myth.]

The opposition of the allegorical force of Ahab's confrontation with an evil Nature and Ishmael's immersion into the dynamic natural system allows for the exploration of universal questions of fate, destiny, and human nature, but it also traces skeins of the underlying design of the novel. Both Ahab and Ishmael build and shape this structure; it is the course and map of their experience through the fictional world. The central themes of coherence and incoherence express the submerged relationships between what is apparent, responsive, and dramatic, and what is veiled, grounded, and fundamental. Subtle, momentary encounters with aspects of Melville's unifying aesthetic or the experience or assault of some invisible force permeate the structure of the novel: The encounters with ambiguous forms, the experience of clearly organized spaces, the inquiries into the properties of light, the descriptive nature of the line, the meaning of forms, and the representations of life are pictorial ideas that contribute to an understanding of Melville's artistic frame of mind and the novel's seamless design.

In the chapter "Of the Monstrous Pictures of Whales," Ishmael grapples with the aesthetic relationship between form and meaning. On his attempt to capture the whole aspect of the whale propelling itself through its environment, Ishmael states:

> you must needs conclude that the great Leviathan is that one creature in the world which must remain unpainted to the last. True, one portrait may hit the mark much nearer than another, but none can hit it with any very considerable degree of exactness. (*M* 264)

Ishmael acknowledges his doomed attempt to express the full reality of the whale in a single picture-making act. To completely represent the whale would deny Ishmael's organic quality and his implication in an unfathomable depth of complexity. He would exist in a panoptic space directed toward a static picture of nature. The viewer would then know Ishmael, anticipating his language patterns and tracing back his perspectives. Ishmael opposes this fixity and transparency; he journeys into the world with a perpetually incomplete map of reality where every point reveals a counter-revelation and every line reveals a perplexing fold in space and time. What we call Ishmael exists in the interplay between the terrestrial immensity of the novel and our own place behind the dense blocks of words. Ishmael is all about the mysterious map of self. The more contradictions the center of consciousness embodies in his language-making act, the greater chance we share in his discovery and contact at the horizon. (...)

Ishmael constantly struggles to grasp a picture of the whale. His activity in the novel, his involvement at every turn, position, and event, builds a system of perspectives that create a world reflective of his own special fascination. This immersion in the world of the novel creates an internal horizon—the sum of a body of various interpenetrating points of view reflecting the whole being of the subject. In *Phenomenology of Perception*, Maurice Merleau-Ponty writes of this emerging phenomenal horizon:

> But the system of experience is not arrayed before me as if I were God, it is lived by me from a certain point of view; I am not the spectator. I am involved, and it is my involvement in a point of view which makes possible both the finiteness of my perception and its opening out upon the complete world as a horizon of every perception.[2]

Ishmael's draw to the horizon embodies the force of his being and becoming in the novel. His textual activity works to complete the picture of the whale at the same time that it shows the whale's otherworldliness—its ungraspable life force which disperses the picture-making act across the whole continuum of human experience. In the chapter "Cetology," Ishmael envisions the monumentality of his project to classify all that is known of whales, likening the attempt to the grand architects' construction of an unrivaled monumental cathedral:

> Finally: It was stated at the outset, that this system would not be here, and at once perfected. You cannot but plainly see that I have kept my word. But I now leave my cytological System standing thus unfinished, even as the great Cathedral of Cologne was left, with the crane still standing upon the top of the uncompleted tower. For small erections may be finished by their first architects; grand ones, true ones, ever leave their copestone to posterity. God keep me from ever completing anything. This whole book is but a draught—nay, but the draught of a draught. Oh, Time, Strength, Cash, Patience! (*M* 145)

According to *The Oxford English Dictionary*, the word *system* was adopted from the Greek word susthma, meaning an "organized whole." This definition of system equally describes the intent of the architect of the cathedral of Cologne and the naturalist's attempt to table all the known varieties of whales. To the medieval architect, the cathedral houses a higher spiritual plane of existence—a glimpse into the magnificence of God. For the naturalist, the table represents a coherent system of distinctions based on certain key physical characteristics. As a whole, the table represents an empirical knowledge of nature—a way to organize and name a diverse field of life. Yet the incompleteness of Ishmael's system, leaving the "copestone to posterity," reveals a cautious hesitancy on Ishmael's part to actualize in language a complete account of nature. If Ishmael were to realize this system, the chapter would be a prison and the world of the novel a place of rigid empiricism. Ishmael carries with him an underlying belief (if not the same faith Ahab holds in his vertical quest) in a primary and essential secret strength of things. He possesses an aesthetic that is not limited or centralized, but emergent and experiential.

NOTE

2. Maurice Merleau-Ponty, *Phenomenology of Perception*, trans. Colin Smith (London: Routledge and Kegan Paul, 1962), 304.

—Shawn Thomson, *The Romantic Architecture of Herman Melville's Moby-Dick* (Associated University Presses, 2001).

Christopher Sten on The Epic Tale of the White Whale

[Christopher Sten is a Professor at George Washington University. He has written *Sounding the Whale: Moby-Dick as Epic Novel*, *The Weaver God, He Weaves: Melville and the Poetics of the Novel* and he edited *Savage Eye: Melville and the Visual Arts*. In this essay, he compares Moby-Dick to other epics and studies the problems facing the heroes.]

1. The Burial of the Dead

Like the *Divine Comedy*, *The Waste Land*, and other spiritual epics, *Moby-Dick* opens with its hero in a fallen state of emotional torpor and confusion. Starting his story before his transforming experience on the *Pequod*, Ishmael says he is like a spiritually dead man in a spiritually dead land, seeking the relief of the condemned everywhere. He has grown weary of existence, as one does when his youth is spent and he finds himself, as Dante said at the start of his story, "In the middle of the journey of our life." He experiences depression, morbidness, even thoughts of suicide, and he hungers for change or escape.

Like Ahab, Ishmael suffers from a malaise or schism in the soul, an aggression so intense as to prove deadly to himself and others. As Ishmael confesses, it is only by holding to "a strong moral principle" that he can keep himself from "deliberately stepping into the street, and methodically knocking people's hats off." Whenever he finds himself overtaken by such an urge, he knows it is "high time to get to sea as soon as I can." However, whether this is to be viewed as a still surer means of realizing a deep-seated death wish or as an alternative to it, a means of regaining his health, Ishmael himself seems a little unsure. Going to sea, he says equivocally, "is my substitute for pistol and ball."[15] Even if he himself is unsure, his unconscious knows there must be a dying to the world before there can be a rebirth. That is the only way one can ever hope to overcome the death of the spirit. Ahab's example attests to that by his failure, as Ishmael's example does by his success. For the hero to come back as one reborn, filled with creative energy, as Ishmael does when he returns to tell his tale at the end, he must first give up the world and everything in it.

It is significant, but not widely recognized, that Ishmael is not alone in his suffering, that he is a representative figure or exemplary hero. "If they but knew it," he writes, "almost all men in their degree, some time or other, cherish very nearly the same feelings towards the ocean with me," and as proof he has to look no further than his own fellow "Manhattoes." Everywhere he looks, on a dreamy Sunday afternoon, he sees "crowds of water-gazers," thirsting for the adventure that will free them from the land and the deadly routine of their lives. All of them, "thousands upon thousands of mortal men fixed in ocean reveries," hunger for that deeper, vivifying knowledge of the spirit that going to sea makes possible. "Meditation and water," Ishmael explains, "are wedded forever" because, as the Greeks were the first to learn, introspection is the way to self-understanding (3–4). However, as the example of Narcissus warns, such inwardness can be a dangerous business; it must not lead simply to a love for the self or a fascinated preoccupation. It has to be conducted as an active search for and testing of the self; it has to involve a trial. Few people get beyond the stage of being weekend water-gazers because they are afraid of the challenge of the new, afraid of what the unfamiliar might hold. They thus remain among the dead, "victims" whom one day a more adventurous soul, like Ishmael, will come back to try to rescue, and so on, in an endless cycle.

What distinguishes Ishmael from these more timid Manhattanites is simply that he accepts the call to the sea. He does so, to be sure, without full understanding of what he is doing or why, but he is the sort of man who lives intuitively and knows to trust his inner promptings wherever they might lead him. Because the episodes in his journey represent trials of the spirit, psychological trials, his passage is inward as much as it is across land or water—"into depths where obscure resistances are overcome," as Campbell explains, "and long lost, forgotten powers are revivified, to be made available for the transfiguration of the world."[16]

In *Moby-Dick* this inner realm is of course represented by the sea, a universal image of the unconscious, where all the monsters and helping figures of childhood are to be found, along with the many talents and other powers that lie dormant within every adult. Chief among these, in Ishmael's case, is the complicated image of the Whale itself, which is all these things and more and also serves as the "herald" that calls him to his adventure. At the end of chapter 1, "Loomings," with its promise of some distant, portentous engagement, Ishmael reveals that his chief motive for wanting to go whaling "was the overwhelming idea of the great whale himself." But that he is responding as much to a lure from within the self as from without is suggested in the final lines of this opening chapter, when he asserts that, having examined his motives and finding the idea of going whaling to his liking, "the great flood-gates of the wonder-world swung open, and in the wild conceits that swayed me to my purpose, two and two there floated in my inmost soul, endless processions of the whale, and, midmost of them all, one grand hooded phantom, like a snow hill in the air" (7). For Melville's hero, this phantom whale that is later incarnated as the great White Whale is the beginning and the end, and it represents all the instinctual vitality locked deep within the self. It is in this sense that the Whale is synonymous with "the ungraspable phantom of life" that is "the key to it all" (5).

Because the way of the hero is through a strange realm filled with danger and hardship, he requires the help of a guide or wisdom figure, some master of the world beyond who can provide the kind of assistance that, to the neophyte, seems magical. As in any initiatory experience, the novice has to be instructed in the rules of the game and have the way pointed out to him. Also, usually the guide supplies a charm or fetish that will serve to ward off danger or insulate the hero from the dark forces unleashed during this process. While the guide is sometimes a woman, like Beatrice in Dante's vision, more typically it is a man, as in the *Divine Comedy* again, where Virgil assumes the role in the early stages. So in *Moby-Dick* Ishmael is guided through the early episodes of his journey by the masterful harpooner and mystagogue, Queequeg, a deeply if comically religious man whose home is a mythical island called Kokovoko. In keeping with such mysterious figures generally, Queequeg is both protective and forbidding, nurturing and threatening, like the complex powers of the unconscious that he symbolizes.[17]

NOTES

15. *Moby-Dick* 3. Subsequent references to *Moby-Dick* are to the Hayford, Parker, and Tanselle edition.

16. Campbell, *Hero with a Thousand Faces* 29.

17. Ibid. 69–73.

—Christopher Sten, *Sounding the Whale: Moby-Dick as Epic Novel* (Kent State University Press, 1986).

BAINARD COWAN ON THE FAITHFUL FORESHADOWING

[Bainard Cowan is an Associate Professor of English at Louisiana State University. He has written *Exiled Waters: Moby-Dick and the Crisis of Allegory*. In this excerpt, he looks at how religious beliefs have a role in *Moby-Dick*, and faithful foreshadowing in the novel.]

The passage in Jeremiah refers to a legend in the time of exile according to which Rachel's voice was heard weeping near the traditional locale of her tomb. She was considered the ancestress of the nation of Israel, and her tears thus stand not for a private or familial grief but for the uprooting of an entire people. The verse in Jeremiah is quoted by Matthew after he gives the account of the massacre of the innocents under Herod: "Then was fulfilled that which was spoken by Jeremy the prophet" (Matt. 2:17). While narrating an incident just before the encounter with the *Rachel*, Ishmael refers to the massacre of the innocents: "the watch—then headed by Flask—was startled by a cry so plaintively wild and unearthly—like half-articulated wailings of the ghosts of all Herod's murdered Innocents" (p. 428). Though the Manxman later identifies these cries as those of the *Rachel*'s drowned crewmen, Ishmael discerns that they are in fact the wails of "some young seals that had lost their dams, or some dams that had lost their cubs" (p. 429).

The motifs leading out from the biblical Rachel thus embrace both man and nature in suffering. The insistence in Matthew that the murder of the innocents was the fulfillment of the figure of Rachel weeping reminds one again that the fulfillment of sacred history can often be negative, for no guaranty of a positive progress through history exists. The wails are taken as one more omen about the doom of the *Pequod*.

The general inefficacy of religious practice to stall the *Pequod*'s fate is evident in the broken rite which the *Delight*'s captain performs on his dead crewman:

> Then turning to his crew—"Are ye ready there? place the plank then on the rail, and lift the body; so, then—Oh! God"—advancing towards the hammock with uplifted

> hands—"may the resurrection and the life—"
>
> "Brace forward! Up helm!" cried Ahab like lightning to his men. (pp. 441–42)

The continuity that religious ritual hopes to effect between the here and the beyond is not allowed to develop. Ahab's will intrudes to break up the sentence that would promise a transition into the next life.

The promise of a smooth passage, in the final analysis, is something that religion cannot fulfill. In his final moment Starbuck asks, "'Is this the end of all my bursting prayers? all my lifelong fidelities?'" (p. 467). And in fact it is. The dream of a foreseeable rescue, a salvation according to plan, is burst. The god that reveals himself at the end is terrible: "Retribution, swift vengeance, eternal malice [are] in his whole aspect" (p. 468) as Moby Dick rams the *Pequod*, the "god-bullied hull" in Ahab's phrase. Even the concentric circles that figured an anagogic peace in the whales' bower now compose a vortex dooming all hands and present nature's final form as universal destruction.

But an invisible, unmanifested god prevails in the last page, a page that makes several gestures to present itself as though it were outside the text: it is printed entirely in italics, is titled "Epilogue," and begins, "The drama's done. Why then here does any one step forth?" (p. 470). And of course it was omitted entirely in the English edition, in a kind of ultimate ambiguity that may never be resolved. But even Melville's contemporary reviewers pointed out that a first-person account could not logically end with the death of all hands. More, however, is involved in the ending than mere survival. The "invisible police officer of the Fates" mentioned in the first chapter apparently once again has jurisdiction, for the sharks seem to have "padlocks on their mouths" and the seabirds "sheathed beaks." This seems a god who operates only in the margins of the text, just where the readable actions of human purpose stop. And he seems to operate only by chance—"It so chanced," Ishmael begins his explanation of how he survived. But as he has asserted in his model of the loom of time, "chance by turns rules either [i.e., fate and free will], and has the last featuring blow at events" (p. 185).

The notion of a saving remnant implies an outline of history that is not a straight, magnificent unfolding—the line figured in the straight wake of the *Pequod*—but is instead a series of last-minute rescues, or, more centrally, a gathering up of survivors after a series of plunges into destruction. In the narrative it is the "devious-cruising *Rachel*" that traces this more erratic line, giving the visual equivalent to the biblical Rachel's unforeseen legacy of unfulfillment and displacement.

In the allegory of interpretation that Ishmael makes of every episode in *Moby-Dick*, the "retracing search" of the *Rachel* also suggests a rereading of the text. And it may provide an answer to what motivates allegorical interpretation. The *Rachel* reverses its course, going over waters it has traversed before, but now it is in search of something it has lost. The son represents the captain's own continuity with the future generation, and as such he represents the idea of continuity with *all* generations. If the father cannot pass on his calling to his son, then the very notion of tradition as a continuity is broken. Deluded as this desire for continuity may be, it is what causes the *Rachel* to reverse its course, without which reversal Ishmael would have drowned, exhausted, at sea. The motive for rereading a text, then, in this allegory of interpretation, may be said to be mistaken; but it is a felicitous mistake.

The *Rachel* is motivated by a desire for origins, for in representing the link of generations the son represents as well the link with the original ancestor. The alternative is the "orphan's" existence of Ishmael. The desire for origins may be equated with what we have called allegorical desire. Allegories could never get under way if from the beginning the allegorist were totally conscious that the gap in being is unbridgeable; he is spurred on by a hope of crossing that gap. In fact it is the sense of loss—what Thomas McFarland has called the "meontic mode" of Romantic writing, a pervasive sense of nonbeing—that finally determines the movement of allegories toward an origin in which they hope they might be saved.[9] Interpretation is born of this desire, for it comes only in a "retracing search" through the text of experience. One may say that interpretation occurs in the hope of finding a continuity of meaning with the origin of meaning in one's experience. Yet what one persistently finds upon rereading—that is, if one's eyes are open—is the unexpected, the radically unconnected element. Ishmael is such a fragment; he is literally "unreadable" in the script of history projected by the *Rachel.* The "Miracle," then—what is truly unexpected and unaccountable—is that Ishmael is taken on board. He becomes part of a text he has radically altered by his mere existence; the text is saved by the realization that it cannot be a prescription, a script, for history.

NOTE

9. Thomas McFarland, "The Place Beyond the Heavens: True Being, Transcendence, and the Symbolic Indication of Wholeness," *Boundary* 2, VII (Winter, 1979), 283–319. Joel Fineman links allegory with the desire for origins in "The Structure of Allegorical Desire," unpublished paper given at the English Institute, 1979.

—Bainard Cowan, *Exiled Waters: Moby-Dick and the Crisis of Allegory* (Louisiana State University Press, 1982).

WILLIAM B. DILLINGHAM ON MARTYRDOM

[William B. Dillingham is a Professor at Emory University. He has written *An Artist in the Rigging: The Early Work of Herman Melville*, and *Melville's Later Novels.* In this essay, he looks at the characters heading for martyrdom in *Moby-Dick.*]

Those predestined for this martyrdom grow in stature as they sail perilously in the howling infinite. But the closer they get to truth, the farther away it is. The more they perceive, the narrower becomes their vision. The more they crave perfection, the more they contribute to imperfection. As they become independent of the forces that debase and enslave ordinary mortals, they are caught up in the insidiousness of cosmic circularity, never to be released. The more they become like a god, the greater their capacity for suffering. The story of Pip, the cabin boy in *Moby-Dick*, is a paradigm of the hero's "ocean-perishing" and apotheosis. After he jumps from a boat, Pip is left alone for several minutes in the open sea. When he is finally picked up, he is mad. His madness is the result of feeling the loneliness which the searching hero inevitably experiences:[5] "But the awful lonesomeness is intolerable. The intense concentration of self in the middle of such a heartless immensity, my God! who can tell it?" Accompanying this intensified loneliness and contributing to his madness is a vision of the inner workings of the universe. He was "carried down alive to wondrous depths, where strange shapes of the unwarped primal world glided to and fro before his passive eyes; and the miser-merman, Wisdom, revealed his hoarded heaps; and among the joyous, heartless, ever-juvenile eternities, Pip saw the multitudinous, God-omnipresent, coral insects, that out of the firmament of waters heaved the colossal orbs. He saw God's foot upon the treadle of the loom, and spoke it; and therefore his shipmates called him mad. So man's insanity is heaven's sense."[6]

Literally Pip perhaps sees some form of coral when he goes under the water. Symbolically it is the vision which awaits such heroes as Taji and Ahab in apotheosis. From diving deeply into the howling infinite, as Ishmael says in "The Lee Shore," one's humanity perishes, but from the experience comes such knowledge as only the gods possess. The creation of coral (and especially of a coral reef) "out of the firmament of waters" suggests the creation of the universe and the repetitious activity of those "multitudinous, God-omnipresent" forces that have continued since creation.[7] The heart of the vision, however, is what they have created—the "colossal orbs"—merely circles upon circles upon circles.[8]

The state of independence which Melville's hero finally reaches produces three closely related attitudes in him: (1) He pays little attention to the laws and dogmas of the world which ordinary people follow; they are generally beneath his consideration, and he does not act as he does to obey laws or because he is afraid of punishment if he breaks them. (2) He has developed a singleness of purpose which frees his conscience of pangs which an ordinary man might feel. Ahab, for example, is not guilt-ridden because he has to commit certain acts against humanity. To Taji also, all things are subordinate to the central pursuit. (3) Consequently such heroes feel free to make use of the world around them in any way that will help them to be about their appointed task.

These three characteristics of psychological freedom follow precisely the three "parts" of true "liberty" which John Calvin discussed and analyzed in his *Institutes of the Christian Religion.* First, "believers ... must rise above the law," he wrote, "and think no more of obtaining justification by it. For while the law ... leaves not one man righteous, we are either excluded from all hope of justification, or we must be loosed from the law...."[9] Secondly, "the soul must previously be divested of every other thought and feeling" except love of God, and "*all its powers collected and united on this one object*" (italics mine).[10] If this is truly done, one's conscience is not encumbered with petty guilts and regrets. Finally, "the third part of this liberty is, that we are not bound before God to any observance of external things which are in themselves indifferent, but that we are now at full liberty either to use or omit them. The knowledge of this liberty is very necessary to us; where it is wanting our consciences will have no rest...."[11] Knowingly or not, Melville was using a Calvinistic framework to arrive at his own unique final vision (which is anything but Calvinistic).

This tragic vision of man in the howling infinite owes a great deal in several other respects—perhaps more than Melville would have cared to admit—to the teachings of Calvin. Melville was brought up and baptized in the Dutch Reformed Church. Although he rejected its dogma (as he did every other kind) and at times reacted strongly against its narrowness, it was nevertheless one of the most important influences of his youth.[12] His specific beliefs about God are more difficult to pin down than the exact meanings of the white whale he created; it is probably just as wrong to view him as an orthodox Calvinist as it is to see him as a bitter and consistent God-hater. He may not have believed in Calvinism at all, but what he *did* believe—as reflected in the first five novels—bears enough resemblance to Calvin's theology as to suggest its derivation from that system of religious thought "from whose visitations, in some shape or other," he wrote, "no deeply thinking mind is always and wholly free."[13]

5. Pip is not himself a searching hero, of course. What happens to him, however, is described in language which applies to such heroes as Taji and Ahab.

6. *Moby-Dick*, p. 347.

7. The coral polyps engage in a strange and wonderful form of creativity as they take from the "firmament" of the sea calcium carbonate and turn it into pure limestone, which is deposited to make their own circular (or tubular) shells and hence the circular coral reefs.

8. For a perceptive treatment of Pip's experience as well as the phenomenon of time in Melville, see Paul Brodtkorb, Jr., *Ishmael's White World: A Phenomenological Reading of Moby-Dick* (New Haven, 1965). Brodtkorb and I disagree, however, on the issue of transcending time. While it is my contention that in Melville's works the hero cannot, even through madness, break out of time, Brodtkorb maintains that "descent, unlike ascent, can finally break the chain of time, process, and circular motion.... In the end, successfully to escape circular horizontality is either to die or to go mad" (p. 41).

9. *Institutes of the Christian Religion*, trans. Henry Beveridge (London, 1953), II, 131.

10. Ibid., II, 133.

11. Ibid., II, 134.

12. For discussions of this influence, see Newton Arvin, *Herman Melville* (New York, 1959); William Braswell, *Melville's Religious Thought* (Durham, 1943), William H. Gilman, *Melville's Early Life and Redburn* (New York, 1951), Lawrance Thompson, *Melville's Quarrel with God* (Princeton, 1952), and Yvor Winters, *Maule's Curse* (Norfolk, Conn., 1938). A recent treatment of Melville's indebtedness in *Moby-Dick* to certain concepts of Calvinism is T. Walter Herbert, Jr., "Calvinism and Cosmic Evil in *Moby-Dick*," *PMLA*, LXXXIV (1969), 1613–19. Herbert's focus is different from my own: he argues that Ahab is Calvin's "reprobate" attacking the Calvinistic God.

13. "Hawthorne and His Mosses," in *Billy Budd and Other Prose Pieces* (London, 1924), p. 129.

—William B. Dillingham, *An Artist in the Rigging: The Early Work of Herman Melville* (University of Georgia Press, 1972).

PLOT SUMMARY OF

Pierre, or The Ambiguities

Written the year after *Moby-Dick*, *Pierre, or The Ambiguities*, expresses Melville's frustrations as the inward and outward writer. Dealing with controversial issue such as incest, and outwardly snubbing the literary establishment, *Pierre* was quickly dismissed by the critics, and sold poorly.

'Easy for man to think like a hero; but hard for man to act like one' (p. 202) is the thought that sums up the story of Pierre Glendinning, as told in Herman Melville's *Pierre*. Pierre, a young man of 19, wealthy, attractive and intelligent, spends his time reading, enjoying his mother's company, and wooing his fiancée Lucy Tartan. Although not of noble birth, Pierre enjoys the admiration and respect usually associated with nobility. In reference to this implied nobility Pierre jokes about being 'Romeo' (a foretelling of his tragic fate) to which his mother responded that he is 'no Romeo' as he would be marrying a 'Montague' in Lucy Tartan. Pierre and his mother Mary enjoy an oddly close relationship. The two playfully refer to each other as brother and sister, as Pierre waits on her, and she dresses for him as though he were a suitor. He is by all accounts a delightful young man whose enchanted life changes when he meets Isabel Banford.

Isabel, a woman working at a nearby farm, faced a harsh childhood spent isolated in a lunatic asylum. Believing that fate has brought them together, she writes to Pierre telling him she is his half-sister. She recounts the tale of her unhappy childhood and difficult upbringing and describes her few brief visits with her father. Pierre, remembering how his father spoke of a daughter while delirious in his dying days, believes Isabel's story and is determined to care for her. His inexplicable devotion to Isabel causes Pierre to break off his engagement to Lucy Tartan. However, in order for him to care for and live with Isabel, he devises the story that the two are married—thinking that they can play the role of husband and wife to the outside world, while living together as brother and sister.

The mother-son relationship begins to falter as Pierre initially hides his relationship with Isabel, and his mother, sensing that he is concealing something, withdraws from him. Mary Glendinning, unwilling to accept Pierre's impetuous marriage, orders him out of their home. She is upset that he has marred the family's social standing, and has recklessly disregarded Lucy's feelings. She is so angered by Pierre's abandoning Lucy and ruining the family name, she disinherits him. When she dies a few weeks later, she leaves the entire family fortune to Pierre's cousin Glendinning Stanly.

Pierre and Isabel move to the city with Delly Ulver, a woman disgraced by an illegitimate pregnancy. Pierre expects to be helped by his cousin and childhood friend Glendinning Stanly—the very cousin who inherits what should have been Pierre's birthright. Instead, Stanly refuses Pierre. Pierre also learns that his cousin is courting his former fiancée Lucy. It is hard news to accept—his cousin is essentially living Pierre's life. Facing poverty, and for the first time forced to earn a living, Pierre decides to support his sister with his writing. He works on a novel by locking himself in his room during the day, writing page after page. Isabel supports him and Delly stays on as their servant. Day after day, week after week, month after month Pierre writes. He grows troubled and disillusioned by what his life has become. He finds a home in an office and apartment complex known as 'The Apostles,' which was a former church. It is mostly attorneys in the office space, and intellectuals in the living quarters. Charlie Millthorpe, an attorney-philosopher and childhood friend of Pierre's sets him up in quarters. The odd family unit lives in a 3-room apartment: Pierre's room, Isabel's room, and Delly in the kitchen.

Months after the sudden unforeseen end to their relationship, Pierre recieves a letter from Lucy. She says she would rather live with Pierre and his wife, than live without him. Her love for Pierre is so great that she is willing to give up a normal life, just to be near him. Pierre aches for Lucy and agrees to let her live in the apartment with him, Isabel and Delly—making Isabel very upset and jealous. She then begins to act more like a wife and less like a sister toward Pierre asking him, 'Am I not enough for you?' She appears jealous of Lucy's beauty and kind manner and fears she will lose Pierre. These fears are magnified by visits from Lucy's brother and suitor Glendinning Stanly. Lucy's mother visits too, trying to persuade Lucy to come home and leave Pierre—calling Isabel a fool for allowing the bizarre arrangement.

The strain of writing and the stress of his home life wear away at Pierre's fragile spirit. As the months go by, Pierre's pleasant outlook becomes dark, angry and hostile. Pierre's growing distemper is aided by the arrival of two letters. In the first, his publisher rejects his manuscript and demands repayment for his writing advances calling him a swindler and a blasphemer (a sly joke as Melville was having trouble selling *Pierre* to his publisher). The second letter is from his cousin, Glendinning Stanly and Lucy's brother Frederic Tartan, calling him a liar. Angered by this second letter, he pilfers a gun and goes out in search of his cousin. When he encounters his cousin he shoots and kills him. With Glendinning Stanly's death, Pierre is arrested. The two women who love Pierre visit him in his cell, and as critic George Washington Peck phrased it, "there is a terrific amount of dying and the usual vial of poison makes its appearance."

LIST OF CHARACTERS IN

Pierre, or The Ambiguities

Pierre Glendinning is the main character in *Pierre*. He is 19, wealthy, engaged to be married, and is the center of his mother's life. His fortune changes when he encounters Isabel, his half-sister. He tries to do what he thinks is right, and destroys the lives of everyone close to him.

Mary Glendinning is the mother of Pierre. She is haughty, beautiful and expects great things from her son, whom she adores. She is bitterly disappointed when he breaks his engagement, and forces him out of the family mansion and writes him out of her will and her life. She dies a short time later without making peace with her only child.

Glendinning Stanly is Pierre's cousin and childhood friend. He does not help Pierre when Pierre leaves his mother to support Isabel. Glen inherits Pierre's mother's estate and courts his former fiancée. Glen is eventually killed by Pierre in a murderous rage.

Lucy Tartan is Pierre's fiancée and soul mate. He breaks her heart by calling off their engagement. Lucy tells Pierre she would rather live with him and his wife, than live without him. She dies in a prison cell with Pierre and Isabel after taking poison.

Mrs. Tartan is Lucy's mother, a matchmaker. The match of her beautiful daughter and the very eligible Pierre pleases her. She is disappointed when her daughter moves in with Pierre and his wife Isabel, and disowns Lucy when she refused to return home.

Frederic Tartan is Lucy's older brother. He and Glendinning Stanly try to persuade Lucy to come to her senses and leave Pierre. He threatens Pierre.

Aunt Llanyllyn is Lucy's aunt. She lives in the country where Lucy stays close to Pierre.

Isabel Banford is Pierre's half-sister. Pierre believes his father had an affair with Isabel's mother, before marrying Mary Glendinning. Isabel was raised by foster parents and had a hard life. She writes to Pierre because she is lonely and looking for her family. She poses as Pierre's wife in order to be with her family.

Mr. Falsgrove is the minister of Mary Glendinning's church. He is pleased by her patronage but is afraid of her. Pierre asks him many moral and ethical questions that he finds impossible to answer, Pierre loses faith in him. Mary Glendinning finds him weak when she needs him during her crisis with Pierre.

Charlie Millthorpe is a childhood friend of Pierre's. He is an attorney who helps Pierre set up in an apartment at the Apostles. While he makes a living as an attorney, it is philosophy that fuels his life.

Plotinus Plinlimmon is the intellectual leader of the Apostles. He has little personal contact with Pierre, but Pierre is greatly affected by Plinlimmon's writing.

Delly Ulver is the maid who lives with Pierre and Isabel in the city. She left the town of Saddle Meadows because she gave birth to an illegitimate child. The baby died but the scandal did not. Pierre thought he would help Delly by moving her out of the village.

CRITICAL VIEWS ON

Pierre, or The Ambiguities

JOHN WENKE ON GOING OVERBOARD

[John Wenke is a Professor at Salisbury State University. He's written *Melville's Muse: Literary Creation & the Forms of Philosophical Fiction* and *J.D. Salinger: A Study of the Short Fiction*. In this excerpt, Wenke discusses all the influences and styles used by Melville in *Pierre*, and how they really do not work well in the novel.]

But Melville's effort was not successful; *Pierre*'s collision of incompatible imperatives guaranteed that the book would rattle foremost among Melville's ostensible "botches" (*Correspondence* 191). In broadest terms, the narrative resembles *all* of Melville's books; it is an amalgam of competing intentions, the predominant genre of domestic romance housing such mismatched tenants as Gothic thriller, Bildungsroman, satire, polemic, and myth, all presented by a narrator who variously affirms and condemns the main character, among many others.[3] In more particular terms, Melville appropriated the florid language of domestic romance, while mocking its artificiality and excess. Not surprisingly, Melville overdid it. To devotees of the form, the narrator's language reads like a vicious parody.

Adding to *Pierre*'s diverse imperatives is Melville's decision to vent his anger by wrenching the nearly completed book in new directions. Higgins and Parker demonstrate that in the course of composition, Melville became shocked by *Moby-Dick*'s mixed reviews and infuriated by Harper's diminutive economic terms for the work in hand ("Flawed Grandeur" 243). Expanding his text by 150 pages, Melville turned Pierre into a juvenile author, shifting the focus from the details of Pierre's relation to Isabel to a dramatization of Pierre's immature attempt to write a "Mature Work" (*Pierre* 282).

In the first half of the book, the narrator remains detached from Pierre's affective situation. His purpose is to render Pierre's decline in fortune. In its most elemental focus, this story radiates from a philosophical dilemma—the disjunction between practical conduct and ideal precept. This issue envelops both the narrator and Pierre in far-reaching explorations of identity, ontology, epistemology, and genealogy. Questions regarding the confluence of conscious and unconscious motives become expressed through conflicts between freedom and fate, contingency and determinism. As Melville revised and expanded the first version of the manuscript, however, the narrator's affective dissociation from Pierre collapses. As Brodhead rightly contends, "Melville is never more personally involved, or, indeed, more in earnest in his novels than he is in *Pierre*" (*Hawthorne* 165). In the second half, the narrator's earlier examination of Pierre's philosophical problem gives way to the narrator's fervid, self-reflexive excursions on such issues as the failure of philosophy, the nature of the compositional process, and the horrors of the publishing marketplace. In Pierre's expanded story the narrator vents Melville's outrage. As the narrator admits, "[I]t is impossible to talk or to write without apparently throwing oneself helplessly open" (259).

Pierre; or, The Ambiguities incessantly delineates the activity of two minds, as exemplified by the narrator's presentation of, and his increasing involvement with, the exigencies of Pierre's "choice fate." In this "philosophically dramatic and dramatically philosophical novel,"[4] Melville peels back layer upon layer of social and psychological surface and thus extends the ontological and epistemological preoccupations of *Moby-Dick*, especially insofar as metaphors of "depth" evoke psychological and philosophical complexes. Pierre's disaster derives from his narcissistic compulsion to project psychological apprehension as extrinsic philosophical truth.

NOTES

3. For discussions of *Pierre* and multiple forms, especially satire, see Braswell, "Early Love Scenes" 212; Stern, *Fine Hammered Steel* 162; Milder, "Melville's 'Intentions'"; and also Brodhead, who argues, "The odd combination of straightforwardness and secret mockery inherent in his handling of the style, characters, and characteristic situations is evidence of [Melville's] ambivalence, his desire both to make use of this genre and to assert his independence from it" (*Hawthorne* 164).

4. An anonymous commentator in 1926 writes, "Melville, it is supposed, has

been re-discovered recently. Actually, folk here rave hysterically about 'Moby Dick,' principally, and apparently lack the wit to know that 'Pierre' is one of the most important books in the world, profound beyond description in its metaphysic: in fact, I believe that you yourself would find something to keep your mind hard at work for many a day if you read that philosophically dramatic or dramatically philosophical novel, for it is a philosophical novel, reaching to heaven and down to hell in its march to a tragic culmination." (Higgins and Parker, *Critical Essays on Melville's* Pierre 117, emphasis in original.)

—John Wenke, *Melville's Muse: Literary Creation & the Forms of Philosophical Fiction* (Kent State University Press, 1995).

H. Bruce Franklin on Savior becomes Destroyer

[H. Bruce Franklin is a Professor at Rutgers University. He has written *The Wake of the Gods: Melville's Mythology*, *Future Perfect: 19th Century American Science Fiction*, *MIA: or Mythmaking in America* and *Prison Writing in 20th Century America*, among others. In this excerpt, he demonstrates how Pierre tries to be a Savior to everyone in his world but instead destroys life as they know it.]

The story of Pierre, the hero of *The Ambiguities*, is the story of a Christian youth, who, by trying to become symbolically and ethically a new Christ, becomes symbolically and ethically a pagan god; who, in trying to be a savior, becomes the destroyer of all that he tries to save.

The story opens by showing Pierre in a pastoral paradise (his hereditary country estate, Saddle Meadows) and in an idyllic romance (with Lucy). With the arrival of Isabel, probably Pierre's illegitimate half-sister, all idylls end. Pierre faces his central ethical problem: should he publicly avow his sister and give her the love which his father's sins have denied her? If he does, he knows that he will thereby disgrace his father and destroy his mother. He believes that the only answer to his problem is to avow Isabel but not as a sister. This, he realizes, will destroy Lucy, but he sees the "all-including query" as "Lucy or God?" He decides to save everybody except Lucy by pretending to marry Isabel and then taking her to the city. Pierre thus leaves his conventional and conventionally pious mother in order to uphold the name of his dead, unconventional, sinning father (whom he had previously regarded as a kind of god); thus he rejects the fair, virtuous, and innocent Lucy, who seems to represent Heaven, in order to accept completely the mysterious dark lady, Isabel, who seems to represent Nature; he abandons his country paradise and enters the hellish city; he renounces society, law, and custom to follow what seems to him the transcendent ethic of Christ. The central irony develops when Pierre, by embracing what seems Christ's message coming from his heart, finds himself incestuously embracing his sister.

In *Moby-Dick* the evils of the world are largely physical, and the ravening sea and the monsters it contains immediately suggest large symbolic values. Because evil in *Pierre* is largely social and ethical, large symbolic values do not grow so naturally out of its action. Yet the symbolism of *Pierre* is ponderous. In fact, because the symbolic action is often too heavy for the physical action, the book often breaks down and its language flies out of control. But the symbolic action itself remains intact.

Pierre; or, The Ambiguities is symbolically the other side of the *Moby-Dick* coin. Ahab begins his hunt by creating the myth of the White Whale; Pierre begins by seeing his only myth destroyed. Ahab succeeds in making all evil "practically assailable" in the White Whale; for Pierre, though "he had bitter cause for quarrel," "there was none to strike." Ahab could at least dart harpoons into a demon monster of the sea; Pierre can only shoot down his own cousin on a pavement in the stony city. Ahab rules a world as a mythic figure, and he leads this world through his myth into destruction; Pierre is impotently cast out, thrown down, imprisoned, and destroyed by the world. *Moby-Dick*, the sea story, moves toward the symbolic demon who glides through the seas of life; *Pierre*, the land story, grinds incessantly among symbolic rocks. On the sea, Ahab shouts at his God in the roaring Typhoon; on the land, Pierre finds that "Silence is the only voice of our God," that those who think they have heard from this God are as absurd "as though they should say they had got water out of stone; for how can a man get a voice out of silence?"

Because *Pierre* is a land story, taking place in a world in which

God is a stony silence, it uses rocks and stones for its chief symbols, for its title, and for its title character. Pierre, the stone of the title, begins as a follower of Peter, and then becomes gradually more and more identified with a real stone. First he submits himself to the "Memnon" or "Terror Stone," a huge balancing rock which serves the function of a *logan*, a huge Druidic balancing rock. This commits him to Isabel and his renunciation of the Saddle Meadows paradise. Following all but two of the major events in the novel, Pierre sees himself in a dream vision metamorphosed into a huge rock, Enceladus, the heaven-defying Titan. And finally, entombed in a stone prison, he becomes in all respects a rock. (...)

The institutions of this world are conceived of in stony terms, and they seek to embody themselves in terms of stone. After "hereditary beliefs, and circumstantial persuasions" crumble, "the fair structure of the world must ... be entirely rebuilded again, from the lowermost corner stone up"; this process is symbolized in the city's stony hell by the Apostle's Tower, which was originally designed as a "supplemental edifice" to the abandoned church, like the church itself "to be promiscuously rented to the legal crowd": "But this new building very much exceeded the body of the church in height. It was some seven stories; a fearful pile of Titanic bricks, lifting its tiled roof almost to a level with the top of the sacred tower." This tower is also a symbol of the central structural principle of *Pierre*, the metamorphosis of Pierre himself from a holy temple to a fearful mass of Titanic stone.

Pierre begins as an innocent child in the little ordered paradise of his family's estate; he ends as an impotent Titan, borne down into hell, but struggling to assault heaven. In his dream vision at the end he sees himself as Enceladus, an uncarved mass of stone, half-buried in rocky earth, threatening with his armless trunk to batter the heaven which has cast him down. His metamorphosis is externally paralleled by his trip from Reverend Falsgrave's "beautiful little marble church" in the country to Plotinus Plinlimmon's pile of Titanic bricks in the churchyard in the stony city. Three internal images embody his metamorphosis—petrifaction, the fallen statue in the ruined temple, and birth. (...)

Only Isabel is explicitly exonerated from Pierre's petrifaction. First the narrator says that the terrors of Isabel's face are "not those of Gorgon." Later, when Isabel asks "is my face Gorgon's?" Pierre answers, "Nay, sweet Isabel; but it hath a more sovereign power; that turned to stone; thine might turn white marble into mother's milk." Isabel, to whom the solid physical world seems unreal and who makes it seem unreal to Pierre also, in one sense causes Pierre himself to dissolve. Pierre's final cry to her shows in what sense she might turn white marble into mother's milk: "Girl! wife or sister, saint or fiend! in thy breasts, life for infants lodgeth not, but death-milk for thee and me!—The drug!" Isabel's milk dissolves Pierre's identity, leaving only his stony body in his stony hell.

Placed against the country-raised Isabel, who dissolves reality, whose symbols are water and vegetative nature, is Lucy, who was born "among brick and mortar in a sea-port," who comes to represent the purity, the pure sterility, and the solidity of marble. When Pierre tells Lucy of his "marriage," she is described as a "snowy, marble statue"; later, she is called "so marble-white," a "marble girl"; she has become the replacement of what previously stood in the marble shrine of Pierre's heart, "the perfect marble form of his departed father; without blemish, unclouded, snow-white, and serene; Pierre's fond personification of perfect human goodness and virtue".

—H. Bruce Franklin, *The Wake of Gods: Melville's Mythology* (Stanford University Press, 1963).

James Duban on Pierre's Intuition

[James Duban is a Professor of English at the University of North Texas. He wrote *Melville's Major Fiction: Politics, Theology and Imagination*, *The Nature of True Virtue: Theology, Psychoanalysis and Politics in The Writings of Henry James, Sr., Henry James, Jr., and William James*. In this essay, he studies the transcendental thoughts found in *Pierre*.]

Pierre, we are told, defies this Transcendental assumption by showing that "the only way God's truth and man's truth correspond is through their contradictions."[5] Previous studies also suggest that *Pierre* responds to Emersonian notions of "Self-Reliance," "Heroism," and the conjunction of intuition and virtue that constitutes the "moral sentiment."[6] Remaining to be addressed, however, are the ways in which these issues emanated from the Miracles Controversy of 1836–45 and the compatibility of this context with the book's critique of uncompromising virtue.[7] We shall see that *Pierre* plays both ends of the Miracles Controversy against the middle by undercutting perfectionist modes of morality implicit in Transcendental ideas about intuition and by challenging the naiveté of Unitarian assumptions about historical certainty. Also to be explored is the way *Pierre* details the anarchical tendencies of Transcendental intuition, which Melville finally shows to originate in self-serving impulses disguised under the garb of benevolent militancy. Finally, we shall consider the relation of Pierre's decision to become an author to the book's early emphasis on Transcendentalism and incest—and we shall do so mainly in response to scholarship that views the "author" chapters of *Pierre* as either intrusive autobiography or as the self-conscious debasement of art with which Melville highlights fiction's inability to convey absolute "truth."[8] Such scholarship overlooks the connection between Transcendental prophecy and the idea of authorship ("[W]herever and however any one is filled to overflowing with this grand idea of God in the soul of man, he will utter it.... He will be an American Author"[9]), as well as the relationship of such "Young American" self-sufficiency to *Pierre*'s preoccupation with incest. Pierre Glendinning is the product of a Transcendental heritage that contemporary Whig criticism was quick to define as narcissistic and that Herman Melville dramatized as being "incestuous" in its displacement of history and external values with the mind's somewhat "novel" and hermaphroditic utterances.

Melville claimed not to have read Emerson prior to 1849. In that year he attended one of Emerson's Boston lectures, and while visiting the Hawthornes in 1850, "one morning he shut himself in the boudoir & read Mr. Emerson's essays."[10] At least part of what he studied seems echoed in *Pierre*, which a reviewer for the *Athenaeum* mistook for "one of the most diffuse doses of transcendentalism offered for a long time to the public."[11] *Pierre* more obviously satirizes "*the Transcendental Flesh-Brush Philosophy*" (P, 295) and those "amiable philosophers of either the 'Compensation,' or the 'Optimist' school" (P, 277), among whom Emerson—who, in "Compensation," says, "the soul refuses limits, and always affirms an Optimism, never a Pessimism"[12]—must surely be numbered. *Pierre*, moreover, advances that the horological world generally scorns "absurd and all-displacing transcendentals" (P, 262), and particularly the sort of idealistic absolutism that, "challenging [Pierre] in his deepest moral being" (P, 49), causes him to assume a "Christ-like" posture, and to vow to "square myself by the inflexible rule of holy right" (P, 106). Transcending the mere "Imitableness of Christ's Character" described by William Ellery Channing, Pierre seeks, as existing scholarship argues, to participate in the universal incarnation mandated by Emerson's Divinity School Address: "Jesus Christ ... estimated the greatness of man. One man was true to what is in you and me. He saw that God incarnates himself in man, and evermore goes forth anew to take possession of his World." But despite Emerson's demands for "a bold benevolence" and the need to "resist for truth's sake the freest flow of kindness, and to appeal to sympathies far in advance," Melville's narrator aptly shows "those advanced minds, ... in spite of advance, ... to remain ... ill-regulated" (P, 166).[13] This is certainly true of Pierre, who, after ruining both his own and several other lives, betrays a still-lingering allegiance to Emersonian metaphysics. For instance, when he receives letters of rebuke from both his publishers and his enemies, Pierre folds the documents, places one under each shoe, and proclaims, "These are most small *circumstances*; but happening just now to me, become indices to all immensities.... On these I will *skate* to my acquittal!" (P, 357; emphasis added). Emerson, too, believed that

> we live amid surfaces, and the true art of life is to *skate well on them*.... [W]e should not postpone and refer and wish, but do broad justice where we are, by whomsoever we deal with, accepting our actual companions and *circumstances*, however

humble or odious, as the mystic officials to whom the universe has delegated its whole pleasure for us.[14]

Yet, whatever these topical allusions to his Emersonian persuasions, Pierre's enthusiasm in championing the moral sentiment in behalf of Isabel cannot be understood in isolation from Transcendental discourses such as George Ripley's, which spoke of "moral relations ... intuitively perceived." Nor can we ignore the connection between this intuitive moral faculty and the Transcendental quarrel with Unitarian historiography: for in the same paragraph where Emerson discourses upon intuitive perception of the Spirit and the perfectibility of "virtue," he says, "to aim to convert a man by miracles is a profanation of the soul."[15] In response, perhaps, to postulates like these, Plinlimmon takes issue with the chronometrical soul's "so-called intuitions of right and wrong" (P, 211). And against his intuitive certainty of Isabel's claim, Pierre persists in weighing historical evidence reminiscent of the Unitarian apologetics to which Emerson objected when debating Andrews Norton over the place of miracles in religion. But neither the tie between intuition and virtue nor the relation of this to Emerson's quarrel with Unitarian historiography—nor, finally, the way these matters figure in *Pierre*—can be understood without a brief review of the "Miracles Controversy."

NOTES

5. F. O. Matthiessen, *American Renaissance: Art and Expression in the Age of Emerson and Whitman* (New York: Oxford Univ. Press, 1911), p. 471.

6. The most comprehensive account of Melville's encounter with such ideas is Barbara N. Blansett's "Melville and Emersonian Transcendentalism," Diss., Univ. of Texas, 1963, esp. pp. 40, 49, 80, 94–95, 102, 105, 110, 137, 142, 147–48, 161, 175–76, 181–82. Worth noting for its more specific attention to *Pierre*'s encounter with the Divinity School Address is Joseph P. Alaimo's 'A Natural Illusion of American Virtue: Melville's Critique of the Transcendental Hero," Diss., Univ. of Minnesota, 1971, pp. 327–62.

7. In stressing the relation of the Miracles Controversy to uncompromising virtue, I use as a point of departure Michael J. Colacurcio's discussion of *Pierre* in "A Better Mode of Evidence—The Transcendental Problem of Faith and Spirit," *Emerson Society Quarterly*, 54 (1969), 20–22.

8. See Hershel Parker, "Why *Pierre* Went Wrong," *Studies in the Novel*, 8 (Spring 1976), 7–23; Hershel Parker and Brian Higgins, "The Flawed Grandeur

of Melville's *Pierre*," in *New Perspectives on Melville*, ed. Faith Pullin (Edinburgh: Univ. of Edinburgh Press, 1978), pp. 162–96; Nina Baym, "Melville's Quarrel with Fiction," *PMLA*, 94 (Oct. 1979), 918–20.

9. "American Authors" (a review of Emerson's "American Scholar"), *Boston Quarterly Review*, 1 (Jan. 1838), 115.

10. For Melville's assertion that he had not read Emerson prior to 1849, and for his attendance at Emerson's lecture, see *Letters*, pp. 78–79. Melville's use of Hawthorne's library is recorded in Sophia Hawthorne's letter (Autumn 1850) to her mother, first published by Eleanor Melville Metcalf, *Herman Melville: Cycle and Epicycle* (Cambridge, Mass.: Harvard Univ. Press, 1953), p. 91. Christopher W. Sten, in "Bartleby the Transcendentalist: Melville's Dead Letter to Emerson," *Modern Language Quarterly*, 35 (March 1974), 31–32, argues that Melville could have read a copy of *Nature, Addresses, and Lectures* ([1849], in *Works*, I:3–77) that Emerson had sent Hawthorne in September of the year previous to Sophia's letter. More recently, Merton M. Sealts, Jr., in "Melville and Emerson's Rainbow," *ESQ: A Journal of the American Renaissance*, 26 (1980), 67–68, labels Melville's familiarity with this volume inconclusive, though he entertains the possibility that a reference to "superior chronometers" in "The Transcendentalist" (included in *Nature, Addresses, and Lectures*) may have inspired some of Melville's thoughts about "chronometricals and horologicals." All of this is relevant to my argument below, which centers around the compatibility of Emerson's "American Scholar" (also in *Nature, Addresses, and Lectures*) with the "author" chapters of *Pierre*. As I suggest above (chapter II), Melville seems to borrow directly from "The American Scholar" in *Redburn* (late spring and early summer, 1849), though necessarily from a printing prior to the September publication of *Nature, Addresses, and Lectures*. Therefore my discussion will stress the *currency* of Emerson's ideas in contemporary literary journals. I shall, however, follow Sealts ("Melville and Emerson's Rainbow," pp. 63–64, 70–71) in assuming Melville's familiarity, by 1850, with Emerson's *Essays, First Series* (1841) and *Essays, Second Series* (1844).

11. Quoted by Jay Leyda, ed., *The Melville Log*, 2 vols. (New York: Harcourt, Brace, 1951), I:464.

12. *Essays, First Series*, in *Works*, II:122. As William Braswell, in "Melville as a Critic of Emerson," *American Literature*, 9 (Nov. 1937), 330, shows, Melville later wrote of Emerson, "He still bethinks himself of his optimism—he must make that good somehow against the eternal hell itself."

13. Emerson, Divinity School Address, *Works*, I:128–29, 148. Cf. Blansett; Alaimo. Other informative readings of Pierre's moral absolutism include Newton Arvin, *Herman Melville* (New York: Sloane, 1950), 219–32; Milton R. Stern, *The Fine Hammered Steel of Herman Melville* (Urbana: Univ. of Illinois Press, 1957), pp. 150–205; Mary E. Dichmann, "Absolutism in Melville's *Pierre*," *PMLA*, 67 (Sept. 1952), 702–15. For the way that *Pierre*'s subversion of metaphysical and ethical idealism also targets the Platonic tradition that informs Transcendental thought, see the chapter titled "Melville and the Platonic Tradition," in Merton M. Sealts, Jr., *Pursuing Melville, 1940–1980* (Madison: Univ. of Wisconsin Press, 1982), pp. 278–336, esp. 317–25.

14. "Experience" (*Essays, Second Series*), in *Works*, III:59, 60–61; emphasis added.

15. George Ripley, review of James Mackintosh's *General View of the Progress of Ethical Philosophy*, in the *Christian Examiner*, 13 (Jan. 1833), 325 (misnumbered 225); Emerson, Divinity School Address, *Works*, I:132. Both here and below, all attributions to the *Christian Examiner* have been verified using William Cushing's author and subject indices, reproduced in *Research Keys to the American Renaissance*, ed. Kenneth Walter Cameron (Hartford, Conn.: Transcendental Books, 1967). For the largely intuitive, though sometimes "intellectual" perception of the moral sentiment in Transcendental thought, see John Q. Anderson, "Emerson and 'The Moral Sentiment,'" *Emerson Society Quarterly*, 19 (1960), 13–15; Alfred J. Kloeckner, "Intellect and Moral Sentiment in Emerson's Opinions of 'The Meaner Kinds' of Men," *American Literature*, 30 (Nov. 1958), 322–328.

—James Duban, *Melville's Major Fiction: Politics, Theology and Imagination* (Northern Illinois University Press, 1983).

EDWARD H. ROSENBERRY ON FINDING 'HAMLET' AND HUMOR

[Edward H. Rosenberry is a Professor Emeritus at the University of Delaware. He wrote *Melville and the Comic Spirit*. In this selection, Rosenberry explains how readers find humor in the text of Pierre, and a similarity to Shakespeare's Hamlet.]

Pierre, on the other hand, is nearly devoid of the whimsicality of Sterne.[13] Its ambiguous comic quality is to be understood in the light of two other Melvillian favorites, Carlyle and Shakespeare. *Sartor Resartus* is generally credited (or blamed) for the conception of *Pierre*'s grotesque and ironic philosopher and for the elephantine playfulness of style which is one of its most insufferable blemishes. Its obvious central paradigm is Hamlet. Scholars and critics have amply exposed the debt on both the tragic and the low-comic levels.[14] But it was somewhere in between that Melville found and adapted the pivotal ambiguity that gives Pierre its controlling quality. What has been said of *Hamlet*'s comic psychology can be applied with preternatural accuracy to both Melville and his self-imaging hero, Pierre:

> The relation between Hamlet's character and humour is an intimate and deep-laid one ... The tragic predicament in which

> he finds himself forces upon him a policy of dissimulation. He must repress his feelings, hide his thoughts; and thus he is led to express nothing but under a veil, to use hints, riddles, puzzling and mystifying words. His mental life develops a double plane; and the duality of his consciousness is so persistent that it becomes as it were normal.[15]

The ambiguity thus cultivated is an attitude of simultaneous defense and challenge before the world, offering an orthodox interpretation with a built-in petard. Such pathological humor results less in the reader's amusement than in the hero's bitter delight in the physical stimulation of danger, the spiritual stimulation of covert honesty, and the intellectual stimulation of exercising his wit.

This extreme form of humor—tragic, morbid, repellent—characterizes both *Hamlet* and *Pierre*, but with one all-important difference. In Shakespeare the ironic mask is worn by the hero alone and is seen from the outside; in Melville it is worn by hero and author alike and must be seen from the inside. *Pierre* is a Chinese puzzle in which we have, literally, a man writing a bitter book about a man writing a bitter book about a man writing a bitter book. In the resultant mirror image the mood of Hamlet becomes the mood of *Pierre* the book as well as of Pierre the man. The final effect is self-mockery, a spectacle that must embarrass any but the most morbid reader.[16]

The ambiguous comic mood in question is most succinctly described in Redburn's word for it—"demonaic." In *Pierre* it is defined in these terms: "If fit opportunity offer in the hour of unusual affliction, minds of a certain temperament find a strange, hysterical relief in a wild, perverse humorousness, the more alluring from its entire unsuitableness to the occasion..." When we add to this mood its element of "wanton aggression," we have, in effect, the mad defiance of Redburn on the river boat, the "perversity" and "reckless contempt" of Harry Bolton, the hat-knocking temper of Ishmael in the opening chapter of *Moby-Dick*. In short, it is Ishmael's "genial desperado philosophy" shorn of its geniality.[17]

In the total context of Melville's work this humor of perversity has, in addition to its organic ambiguity, an ambiguous potential. It is capable of a positive and a negative expression, a constructive and a destructive, a bright and a dark. In one form or the other, or both, it appears like a signature in most of his writings, frequently marked by specific verbal echoes that return familiarly upon us. In *Israel Potter* the word "demoniac" keeps recurring in connection with the desperate humor it describes. When the luckless soldier of fortune, a satanic concentration of Israel Potter in *The Confidence-Man*, explodes in a burst of "milk-turning" laughter, Melville calls him both a "demoniac" and a "hyena," an epithet he had used for identical purposes in *Mardi* and *Moby-Dick*."[18]

Standing at the bright extreme of the demoniac mood, along with the chastened Ishmael, is the Ethan Allen of *Israel Potter*. "Scornful and ferocious" in captivity, he was yet full of "that wild, heroic sort of levity, which in the hour of oppression or peril seems inseparable from a nature like his; the mode whereby such a temper evinces its barbaric disdain of adversity, and how cheaply and waggishly it holds the malice, even though triumphant, of its foes!"[19] This is the true and admirable Pantagruelism, scornful of fortune but jealous of dignity. It was in this spirit that Melville remembered in his declining years the greatest hero of them all—Jack Chase. In *John Marr and Other Sailors* (1888) he called him "Jack Roy" because he was "king" of the crew, but he is the same manly captain of the main-top his admirer had celebrated in *White-Jacket*:

> *... a gallant, off-hand*
> *Mercutio indifferent in life's gay command.*
> *Magnanimous in humor; when the splintering shot fell,*
> *"Tooth-picks a-plenty, lads; thank, 'em with a shell!"*
> . . . . .
> *Larking with thy life, if a joy but a toy,*
> *Heroic in thy levity wert thou, Jack Roy.*[20]

At the dark pole of perversity it is the self-derisive cynicism of Hamlet that is indulged by Israel Potter, sharing "the reckless sort of half-jolly despair" of the "dismal desperadoes" enslaved in the brickyard, and by Pierre, refusing to proofread his book and "jeering with himself at the rich harvest thus furnished to the entomological critics."[21] Years later Melville wrote his own remorseful commentary on the unwholesome humor of *Pierre*:

Wandering late by morning seas
When my heart with pain was low—
Hate the censor pelted me—
Deject I saw my shadow go.

In elf-caprice of bitter tone
I too would pelt the pelted one:
At my shadow I cast a stone.

When lo, upon that sun-lit ground
I saw the quivering phantom take
The likeness of St. Stephen crowned:
Then did self-reverence awake.[22]

Pierre's favorite books were *Hamlet* and the *Inferno*. The combination is significant, for the whole ambiguous problem of bright and dark with which Melville wrestled so self-consciously from *Mardi* on usually led him, quite unprotesting, straight to Hell.

NOTES

13. Melville borrowed once from *Tristram Shandy* but for noncomic purposes: The Plinlimmon pamphlet is found as casually and lost in precisely the same manner (through a hole in a coat pocket) as the sermon of Yorick which has been suggested as an influence on *The Confidence-Man*. Cf. *P* 14:242, 21:346; *Tristram Shandy* (Modern Library edition), pp. 105, 128.

14. Murray's notes point out numerous comic parallels—e.g., the grave-digger and the landlord of the Black Swan (*P* 13:238). The tragic relations are discussed by S. Foster Damon, "Pierre the Ambiguous," *Hound and Horn*, 2:107–118 (1929). See also Arvin's somewhat broader attribution of low-comic characters to Shakespearean influence: *Herman Melville*, pp. 227–228.

15. Louis Cazamian, "Humour in 'Hamlet,'" *Essais en deux langues* (1938), p. 133 (reprinted from *The Rice Institute Pamphlet*, July 1937).

16. Critics have toyed with this idea for years: see John Freeman, *Herman Melville* (1926), p. 111; and E. L. Grant Watson, "Melville's *Pierre*," *New England Quarterly*, 3:199 (1930). The definitive statements on the subject are by William Braswell: "The Satirical Temper of Melville's *Pierre*," *American Literature*, 7:424–438 (1936), and "Early Love Scenes in Melville's Pierre," *American Literature*, 22:283–289 (1950).

17. *P* 11:218–219, 9:195; *R* 2:13, 44:246. The contrasting moods of Ishmael and Pierre are brilliantly discussed in Sedgwick, *Herman Melville*, pp. 155–157.

18. *CM* 19:107.

19. *IP* 22:241.

20. *Collected Poems*, p. 185
21. *IP* 23:251, *P* 25:400.
22. "Shelley's Vision," *Timoleon* (1891); in *Collected Poems*, p. 233.

—Edward H. Rosenberry, *Melville and the Comic Spirit* (Harvard University Press, 1955).

Edgar A. Dryden on Shakespeare's Influence

[Edgar A. Dryden is a Professor of English at the University of Arizona. He has written critical studies on Melville and Hawthorne. In this essay, he discusses how Melville loves to read and how he writes for his readers.]

Pierre is a book about reading and writing, about the consumption and production of literary texts—a double problem that fascinates Melville from the beginning to the end of his writing career. For unlike some of his romantic contemporaries he does not regard reading as a passive and parasitical activity that is the pale complement of the original and glamourous act of creation itself. Melville is free of the Hawthornian nostalgia for a "Gentle," "Indulgent," appreciative reader who graciously accepts unquestioningly the beautiful tapestry "woven with the best of the artist's skill, and cunningly arranged with a view to the harmonious exhibition of its colours." For Melville the writer is himself originally a reader: indeed his creative powers depend on the depth and breadth of his reading, "spontaneous creative thought" being a process whereby "all existing great works must be federated in the fancy; and so regarded as a miscellaneous and Pantheistic whole." [*Pierre; or, the Ambiguities*. Evanston: Northwestern Univ. Press, 1971, p. 284. All subsequent references to *Pierre* will be from this edition.] The fabric of *Moby-Dick*, for example, is woven more from the threads of the texts that fill Ishmael's library than it is from the lines and ropes of the whaling world. Indeed Ishmael's relation to that world he seeks to represent is that of a reader to a text, and he tries to organize and arrange it as he previously has done his library by establishing a bibliographical system. Productive reading, however, is not an easy or casual activity; "no ordinary letter sorter ... is equal to it." In "Hawthorne and His Mosses," Melville distinguishes between that reader who sees Shakespeare as a "mere man of Richard-the-Third humps, and Macbeth daggers," who responds only to the "popularizing noise and the show of broad farce, and blood-besmeared tragedy," and the more discriminating reader who seeks out the "still rich utterances of a great intellect in repose." In the place of "blind, unbridled" reading Melville proposes a deeply committed one that is capable of discerning those truths that the writer "craftily says," or "insinuates" in his text. As Ishmael demonstrates when he tells the "Town Ho's Story" by "interweaving in its proper place the darker thread [the secret part of the tale] with the story as publicly narrated on the ship," story-telling is a process of representing a dark truth that will only be available to the readers whose response is in the form of deep and probing examination.

At first glance, then, the Hawthorne essay seems equally to celebrate reading and writing, to regard both as distinguished and difficult but nonproblematic activities. Composed during the period when Melville was hard at work on *Moby-Dick*, the essay implies a direct and unambiguous link between Shakespeare and Hawthorne and more importantly, records the positive effects of both writers on Melville. These effects are clearly discernible in the novel he was about to dedicate to Hawthorne. However, important if unacknowledged problems exist in the essay. At the same time that Melville records the way in which the "soft ravishments of [Hawthorne] spin [him] round about in a web of dreams" and celebrates Shakespeare's "great Art of Telling the Truth," he also "boldly condemn[s] all imitation, though it comes to us graceful and fragrant as the morning; and foster[s] all originality, though, at first, it be crabbed and ugly as our own pine knots." The essay, in other words, raises and then ignores the problems of derivation: authority and priority, tradition and the individual talent, literary fathers and sons. But his consideration of these issues is postponed only until *Moby-Dick* is completed, for in *Pierre* Melville focuses on them with an almost desperate insistence.

I

> Dearest Lucy!—well, well;—'twill be a pretty time we'll have this evening; there's the book of Flemish prints—that first we must look over; then, second, is Flaxman's Homer—clear-cut outlines, yet full of unadorned barbaric nobleness. Then Flaxman's Dante;—Dante! Night's and Hell's poet he. No, we will not open Dante. Methinks now the face—the face minds me a little of pensive, sweet Francesca's face—or, rather, as it had been Francesca's daughter's face—wafted on the sad dark wind, toward observant Virgil and the blistered Florentine. No, we will not open Flaxman's Dante. Francesca's mournful face is now ideal to me. Flaxman might evoke it wholly,—make it present in lines of misery—bewitching power. No! I will not open Flaxman's Dante! Damned be the hour I read in Dante! more damned than that wherein Paolo and Francesca read in fatal Launcelot! (*P*, 42)

Woven and entangled in this passage are most of the thematic strands of *Pierre*: the problem of reading; the question of relatedness, of genealogical continuity and intertextuality (family structures and narrative forms); and linking them all the larger issues of repetition and representation. The generative energy of the passage (and the novel) is a story, the "story of the face," a story that Pierre can narrate but cannot read because it exists for him in the form of a "riddle" (P, 37) or "mournful mystery" whose meaning is "veiled" behind a "concealing screen" (P, 41). Nevertheless, he is determined to understand it fully, to confront its meaning, as he says, "face to face" (P, 41). But as the labyrinthine quality of the passage suggests, the meaning of the story is difficult to decipher, and Pierre's attempt to read it will generate a second and even more entangled and problematic narrative, that of the novel itself.

—Edgar A. Dryden, "The Entangled Text: Pierre and the Problem of Reading." (*Boundary* 2, 3, vol. 7, 1979).

C.R.L. James on How *Pierre* was ahead of its Time

[C.R.L. James was a Marxist Theorist and worked for the Socialist Workers' Party while writing and lecturing in the United States. He wrote *Mariners, Renegades & Castaways: The Story of Herman Melville and the World We Live In* while detained for passport violations. Here he examines why *Pierre* was ahead of its time.]

He can feel no passionate love such as he feels for Lucy, because she is his sister. Yet she is the subject of the most ardent and deepest emotions of his soul. She therefore soars out of the realms of mortality and for Pierre becomes transfigured into the highest heaven of Uncorrupted Love.

The old life is behind and this is the vision of the new: Nature, physical magnetism, the sense of history, of space and time, of rejecting social corruption and searching for truth, ethics, i.e., what is the correct thing to do. For a few hours Pierre's soul, cramped by his docile life with his wealthy mother, expands boundlessly. Nor is Pierre just any young man. All his sensations become part of one great central experience, his meeting with Isabel. The personality divided into separate parts, of which the early nineteenth century already was so acutely conscious, is now a totality. (...)

That is the sickness of this generation of intellectuals; not so much that they commit incest but that they preoccupy themselves unceasingly with incestuous desires, father-complex, mother-fixation as the foundation of human personality and human behaviour. As is usual with them (for they do most of the literary work of the world) they transform their preoccupation into a characteristic of the whole world and seek to account through this for the inability of modern man, i.e., themselves, to solve his problems. What Freud discovered at the turn of the century and thought was eternal human nature, was in reality the reaction of the crisis which now has mankind by the throat upon the middle classes and the intellectuals.

That the elements of incestuous desires exist in children from their early associations with their parents seems to be true. But whether these are shed as easily as other childhood diseases or remain to become the refuge of guilt and indecision and fear and shame, that is a social question. What Melville saw was the way in which the traditional, the accepted, the established, however admittedly corrupt, retains its grip on those who want to break with it, or seem to have broken with it,—and the consequences to personality.

As you follow the story of Pierre, you see that whenever Pierre makes a cowardly or dishonest decision, he is almost immediately overwhelmed by the perverse passion he is striving to conquer. Melville does not claim to understand the internal processes whereby Pierre fell into this pit of degradation, but he says if he may venture one superficial reason, it is because Pierre was prepared for it by playing brother and sister with his mother. And that we know was Mrs. Glendinning's method of keeping a grip on her son, i.e., ensuring the continuation of her way of life. There is a passing but suggestive remark on homosexuality: young boys, wealthy and full of spirit, often show the external signs of being in love with one another. But, says Melville, that soon passes off, if everything else goes well with them. It should be noted that in *White-Jacket* Melville mentions homosexuality among the sailors, but it is clear that there it is simple vice, brought on by the fact that they have been away from women for long periods of time. The incestuous desires of Pierre are strictly an intellectual disease. (...)

In that part of the book where he states the case, Melville writes magnificently but once Pierre sets out for New York, Melville's creative power rapidly declines. All that Melville knows is that Pierre is headed for disaster. And he does not care very much how he gets him there.

Such is this remarkable novel, with all its faults, unique, unapproached for a hundred years. As with *Moby-Dick*, the world of 1850–1914 had to be shattered before what Melville was driving at could be seen. Intellectuals like Ishmael would go directly to the working class. Pierre was a different type, the man of ideas and sensitivity. Violently alienated from the old world by its corruption and its selfishness, he would turn to the poor and the humble, seeking to regenerate the world by new discoveries in Truth, and Wisdom and ethical principles. There are none such to be found anywhere. Hence Pierre clung to the old conceptions, could not break once and for all with his father's world. His incestuous desires for Isabel were the only means by which the tempestuous social passions and visions aroused in him would find an outlet. She was half-Glendinning and half-immigrant. It was his only means of reconciling irreconcilable worlds. (...)

Those who read *Pierre* in 1852, needless to say, were scandalized. Many years were to pass before men were educated to believe that incestuous desires were a permanent part of their personalities.

What now happened to Melville is a story very strange, very sad, and yet, as everything about this extraordinary man, very significant for the history of our times.

> —C.R.L. James, *Mariners, Renegades & Castaways: The Story of Herman Melville and the World We Live In* (University Press of New England, 1953, 1978).

Wyn Kelley on the Labyrinth of Life

> [Wyn Kelley teaches at the Massachusetts Institute of Technology. He wrote *Melville's City: Literary and Urban Form in Nineteenth-Century New York*. In this excerpt, he explains how Pierre is making his way through the Labyrinth of Life.]

Pierre makes a remarkable journey through a labyrinth that is conceived, not just in terms of the contemporary city, but in terms of the ancient sources of the modern labyrinth—that is, the labyrinth of Crete. Melville's narrator evokes this labyrinth specifically in the passage that introduces this chapter. It is one of the most puzzling passages in the novel. Pierre, in the midst of making his fateful decision to enter a pretended marriage with his illegitimate sister Isabel, meditates on his extraordinary choice. The narrator suggests that because of his youth Pierre lacks the calm resolve that would foresee the dangers of what he is doing: "That all-comprehending oneness, that calm representativeness, by which a steady philosophic mind reaches forth and draws to itself, in their collective entirety, the objects of its contemplations; that pertains not to the young enthusiast" (175). Instead, Pierre rushes enthusiastically into his "new and momentous devoted enterprise, [ignoring] the thousand ulterior intricacies and emperilings to which it must conduct" (175). With supreme confidence in the rightness of his choice, "this hapless youth [is] all eager to involve himself in such an inextricable twist of Fate, that the three dextrous maids themselves could hardly disentangle him, if once he tie the complicating knots about him and Isabel" (175).

Certainly the narrator's tone warns of the dire consequences of Pierre's entering the moral labyrinth of an assumed marriage with his sister. But in the next sentence, the narrator implies that there are other labyrinths toward which Pierre could or ought to move: "Ah, thou rash boy! are there no couriers in the air to warn thee away from these emperilings, and point thee to those Cretan labyrinths, to which thy life's cord is leading thee? Where now are the high beneficences? Whither fled the sweet angels that are alledged [sic] guardians to man?" (176). This passage implies that Pierre's guardian angels, in directing him *away* from the intricacies and emperilings of his fateful decision, would lead him *toward* another labyrinth, the Cretan labyrinth to which his life's cord is leading him. Whatever path Pierre chooses, then, he is in a labyrinth."[64] The labyrinth depends on his choice.

The emphasis on choice, even a choice attended and aided by fates, angels, and "gods of woe" (179), suggests what for Melville defines the experience of traveling through a labyrinth. A labyrinth is a landscape of choice. The Cretan labyrinth tested a hero's skill and nerve by offering a structure of winding and roundabout paths among which he must find the right way to the center, or heart, of the labyrinth. These paths are called, in the works of Ovid and other classical writers, *ambages*, from the word *ambo*, meaning "two" or "both"; the *ambages* give the traveler a choice between two possible paths. *Ambages* is both a technical term for a labyrinthine structure and also a metaphor for labyrinthine forms of speech or experience:

1. (a) A roundabout or circuitous path, course, etc., meanderings, twists and turns; (b) a roundabout or circuitous movement, wandering to and fro
2. Long-winded, obscure or evasive speech, a circumlocution, digression, evasion
3. Mental confusion or uncertainty. (Doob, 53)

As this definition of the Latin term makes clear, the English "ambiguity" bears a direct linguistic relationship with the structure, experience, and language of the labyrinth. "Ambiguity" in this context means not simply mystery but doubleness, causing doubt or uncertainty about choice. In calling his novel *Pierre, or the Ambiguities*, Melville suggests that Pierre is a man in a labyrinth—wandering, uncertain, and forced to choose between two paths.

It is no accident, then, that Pierre's two great sources of inspiration are Hamlet, who stands on the brink of a choice between being and not-being, and Dante, who begins his *Divine Comedy* by losing his way in the woods and turning to Virgil, himself a poet of the labyrinth, to guide him through the labyrinths of Hell. Both give him courage for "[h]igh deeds" (171); both invite him into the "city of Woe" (168). It is also no accident that Pierre's mind and tongue follow the ambages through which he has chosen to travel. A man of ambiguity, he speaks, as does Melville's narrator, the language of ambiguity—the "long-winded, obscure or evasive speech" of the labyrinth. Clearly, Melville meant his labyrinth to suggest, not just a particular place like the city of New York, but also an ongoing existential condition in a man who makes a momentous decision that involves him thereafter in a perpetually ambiguous state.

But Melville also makes it clear that Pierre's labyrinth, the one to which his life's cord is leading him, is the Cretan labyrinth, and hence invokes the myth of Daedalus, Minos, Theseus, Ariadne, Pasiphaë and her son, the Minotaur. This myth reminds us that someone built the labyrinth, that it did not simply appear. This human agency in the building of the labyrinth is important for our understanding of Pierre's agency in building his, and so I shall review the myth.[65]

The first difficulty in locating human agency in the building of the labyrinth is identifying the builder. Daedalus, of course, designed the labyrinth; but Minos commissioned it, and if Pasiphaë had not loved a bull, Minos would not have wanted one in the first place. The labyrinth Minos had in mind served as a prison, foremost, for the dangerous Minotaur; but Minos also sought to hide the Minotaur, evidence of his cuckoldry and shame, from public view. Later, when he devised the idea of feeding his enemies to the Minotaur, the labyrinth became a slaughterhouse as well. Its intricacy, then, served several purposes: to protect the Minotaur from intruders, to protect the public from the Minotaur, and eventually to create a grisly game or ritual out of the Minotaur's meals. This is the labyrinth that Minos had built, a structure to bolster and protect his own power. But the labyrinth Daedalus built attests to his creative genius in being able to design a structure of wondrous intricacy, a structure that seen from the air rather than from the ground might appear beautiful rather than terrifying. Daedalus also created the labyrinth as a test of heroic skill; the hero who can find his way in the labyrinth deserves a kingdom. Finally, Daedalus made the labyrinth an artifact of desire. It houses the offspring of Pasiphaë's desire for a bull, and it brings Ariadne and Theseus together in their successful conquest of the Minotaur. It suggests Daedalus's alliance with feminine genius, for he gives Ariadne the thread by which she saves Theseus.

At the heart of Minos's labyrinth is power and death; at the heart of Daedalus's, creativity and desire. Both forces are morally ambiguous, however. Minos represents the patriarchal power of the state oppressing young men and maids, but he also upholds marriage and family by punishing Pasiphaë and her son, and strengthens Crete by subjugating Athens. Daedalus represents heroic ingenuity and unfettered desire, but at the same time he is powerless to prevent the human sacrifices and the disasters that threaten Theseus's and Ariadne's love. The labyrinth, then, embodies (among its many meanings) the uneasy union between pure urges—hunger, anger, lust, predation—and social structures: political order, family, and artifice. It is double doubleness.

Without referring again specifically to the Cretan labyrinth, Melville nevertheless implies throughout *Pierre* that the labyrinth—the labyrinth of the city, the novel's labyrinthine plot, Pierre's quest for truth in a labyrinth of experience—has been constructed out of conflicting impulses: it is both a creation of the imagination and an imposition of human choice. Pierre is generally confused about his motives, but at every juncture he makes his choices and creates his labyrinths for himself. By choosing Isabel, Pierre creates a moral, legal, and sexual labyrinth; by attempting a novel that will shatter moral and literary conventions, Pierre constructs a literary labyrinth that he can never get through or beyond; and in entering enthusiastically into a condition of ambiguity, mystery, and misery, he becomes mystified by his own creations. Only when Pierre can see that mystery is something *created*, not accidental, can he penetrate the mystification that surrounds him. By then, however, he has wandered into the path that leads to the prison, the house of crime and passion, rather than into the heart of the labyrinth.[66]

Although in *Pierre* Melville reaches back to mythic and literary labyrinths for inspiration, he also employs some of the narrative structures of the contemporary urban literature, in particular the country–city and aristocrat–pauper contrasts, the rush to ruin, and the ideas of mystery and misery used to represent the city as an overwhelming labyrinth from which the provincial protagonist can never escape. In *Redburn* and *White-Jacket*, Melville used these conventions innovatively, criticizing the provincial protagonist who allows himself to be mystified by the city's mysteries. *Pierre* complicates and deepens this mockery by making it ambiguous, by giving the reader many choices. Thus we see that the conventions are being used, but their meaning is unclear.[67]

NOTES

64. Eric Sundquist suggests that "to descend into the heart of a man like Pierre" is to enter a genealogical labyrinth: "Genealogical source and ethical motive become lost in an inexplicable tangle of obscurity and ambiguity opening out over an abyss, a sarcophagus without a body." *Home as Found: Authority and Genealogy in Nineteenth-Century American Literature* (Baltimore: Johns Hopkins UP, 1979), 161–2.

65. The Cretan labyrinth is somewhat different from the many Christian constructions of the labyrinth, where choice ends once one has entered the labyrinth. See Doob (n. 4) and my "*Pierre* in a Labyrinth: The Mysteries and Miseries of New York," in Robert Milder, ed., *The Evermoving Dawn: Essays in Celebration of the Melville Centennial* (Kent, Ohio: Kent State UP, 1996).

66. A number of critics have located that site of crime and passion in Pierre's and Melville's own sexuality, or his father's sexuality. See Amy Puett Emmers, "Melville's Closet Skeleton: A New Letter About the Illegitimacy Incident in *Pierre*," *Studies in the American Renaissance* (1977): 339–43; and "New Crosslights on the Illegitimate Daughter in *Pierre*," in Brian Higgins and Hershel Parker, eds., *Critical Essays on Herman Melville's "Pierre, Or the Ambiguities"* (Boston: G. K. Hall, 1983), 237–40; Philip Young, *The Private Melville* (University Park, Pa.: Pennsylvania State UP, 1993); James Creech, *Closet Writing/Gay Reading. The Case of Melville's "Pierre"* (Chicago: U of Chicago P, 1993).

67. Reynolds argues: "The second half of the novel is not only about the kind of dark city mysteries and philosophical ambiguities that typified popular sensationalism; it is simultaneously about the contemplation of such mysteries and ambiguities by the reflective American novelist," *Beneath the American Renaissance*, 294.

—Wyn Kelley, *Melville's City: Literary and Urban Form in Nineteenth-Century New York* (Cambridge University Press, 1996).

Richard H. Brodhead on Melville's Creative Process

[Richard H. Brodhead is a Professor of English at Yale University and has written *Hawthorne, Melville and the Novel*. In this essay, he explains Melville's creative process in *Pierre*.]

So many passages in the later books resemble *Mardi* in some way as to suggest that Melville is rewriting rather than writing. As he comes to realize in it, the true significance of *Mardi* is that it is the first draft of all his subsequent works. Not a draft in the sense that it consciously undertakes to produce a rough version of a work whose subject or form is defined, however vaguely, in advance—as we have seen, Melville refuses to build himself in with plans, asserting his right to improvise without constraint. Rather, it is a draft in the sense that, without attempting to foresee what it is a preparation for, it nevertheless gives initial formulation to the work that comes after it—without being directed toward any end, Melville's improvisational act generates themes, thoughts, characters, images, narrative forms, and stylistic features out of which other creations can then be made. In giving him the particular materials and skills that their composition required, and more generally in making him capable of conceiving and expressing them, the writing of *Mardi* made Melville the author who could then go on to write *Moby-Dick*, *Pierre*, and *The Confidence-Man*. To use Keats's words *Mardi* is the form in which the Genius of Poetry in Melville worked out its own salvation. Its spirited performance is the necessary prelude to the mature career of an author who always gained in power by exercising his power—who grew imaginative by exerting his invention, who grew profound by diving after deep thoughts, and who grew creative by engaging in the act of creation.

We have been considering how images and ideas that germinate in *Mardi* reappear in more fully developed forms in Melville's later novels. By way of an epilogue we might note that *Mardi*'s vision of the nature of its own creative act undergoes the same process of maturation. 'Sailing On' and Babbalanja's discourse on the Poet Lombardo are the first drafts of the concluding sections of *Pierre*, the sections treating Pierre's experience as an immature author attempting a mature work. Melville's earlier descriptions of how he was blown off course by a blast resistless and how Lombardo was 'churned into consciousness' are expanded into a full-scale analysis of how through 'a varied scope of reading' and the welling up of 'that bottomless spring of original thought which the occasion and time had caused to burst out in himself' Pierre is 'swayed to universality of thought'. The peculiar impulse of artistic confession, Melville's compulsion to push aside his narrative and share with us directly his personal experience as an author, reasserts itself here: *Pierre*'s comments on authors composing 'paltry and despicable' works, 'born of unwillingness and the bill of the baker', repeat and elaborate on Babbalanja's description of Lombardo's anguished consciousness of his work's imperfections, a work undertaken through 'the necessity of bestirring himself to procure his yams'. Melville also returns to the notion of writing as an act of self-discovery and self-creation, expanding the story of Lombardo's creation of the creative into an even more detailed account of the symbiotic relation between verbal articulation and the generation of creative consciousness:

> that which now absorbs the time and the life of Pierre, is not the book, but the primitive elementalizing of the strange stuff, which in the act of attempting that book, has upheaved and upgushed in his soul. Two books are being writ; of which the world shall only see one, and that the bungled one. The larger book, and the infinitely better, is for Pierre's own private shelf. That it is, whose unfathomable cravings drink his blood; the other only demands his ink. But circumstances have so decreed, that the one can not be composed on the paper, but only as the other is writ down in his soul.

The amazing thing about *Mardi*'s concluding chapters is how well Melville's creative self comes to understand its doings and its needs in them. The wonder of these sections of *Pierre* is that, over the space of only three years, that self has come to know itself so much better—in terms of Melville's letter to Duyckinck they are the twenty-mile step through which his other leg catches up with and outdistances his first's ten-mile step. Thus the Melville who so enthusiastically goes about furnishing *Mardi* with what he is finding in books of literature and philosophy has recognized, by the time he writes *Pierre*, that 'all mere reading is apt to prove but an obstacle hard to overcome', that others' works can only obstruct the author's imagination unless he uses them 'simply [as] an exhilarative and provocative' to his own 'spontaneous creative thought'. Thus too the Melville who rejects all controls on the artist's work except that of the 'one autocrat within—his crowned and sceptered instinct' has discovered, by the time of *Pierre*, the artist's need to learn the discipline of a formal craft: however fine the marble in his mental quarry, Melville writes there, if he is to make a lasting work the young author 'must wholly quit ... the quarry, for awhile; and not only go forth, and get tools to use in the quarry, but must go and thoroughly study architecture'. Above all he recognizes in *Pierre* that the mental stride he took in writing *Mardi* was not a completed movement but 'one of the stages of the transition' of his evolution, that in it he had only initiated the process of discovering a world of mind.

If they reveal a growth of self-knowledge, Melville's rewritings of *Mardi* in *Pierre* also reveal a radical reversal of vision. Thus, developing *Mardi*'s conceit that 'genius is full of trash', Melville writes in *Pierre*:

> it is often to be observed, that as in digging for precious metals in the mines, much earthy rubbish has first to be troublesomely handled and thrown out; so, in digging in one's soul for the fine gold of genius, much dullness and common-place is first brought to light. Happy would it be, if the man possessed in himself some receptacle for his own rubbish of this sort; but he is like the occupant of a dwelling, whose refuse can not be clapped into his own cellar, but must be deposited in the street before his own door, for the public functionaries to take care of. No commonplace is ever effectually got rid of, except by essentially emptying one's self of it into a book; for once trapped in a book, then the book can be put into the fire, and all will be well. But they are not always put into the fire; and this accounts for the vast majority of miserable books over those of positive merit.

Here again the production of inferior work is seen as a stage through which an author must pass on his way to producing superior work, but here this process has costs as well as gains. The trash through the writing of which genius evolves persists as an encumbrance to the emerging artist; by writing it he becomes implicated in producing the mediocre literature in which works of merit are smothered. The image of Lombardo going deeper and deeper into himself is revised even more drastically.

> Yet now, forsooth, because Pierre began to see through the first superficiality of the world, he fondly weens he has come to the unlayered substance. But, far as any geologist has yet gone down into the world, it is found to consist of nothing but surface stratified on surface. To its axis, the world being nothing but superinduced superficies. By vast pains we mine into the pyramid; by horrible gropings we come to the central

room; with joy we espy the sarcophagus; but we lift the lid—and no body is there!—appallingly vacant as vast is the soul of a man!

Here the act of probing discloses not a paradise of creative fullness but the nightmare of a central emptiness.

In these passages we see Melville remaking *Mardi* into the vision of *Pierre*, the vision of the world as an imposture that every effort to escape only deepens one's involvement in. But the difference between these books is less a matter of their metaphysical stances than of their moods. *Pierre* is a book in which the creative impulse has lost faith in its own creativeness. Where *Mardi* images itself as a strong grain ripening into a rich harvest, *Pierre* is haunted by the spectacle of failed maturation—'Oh God, that man should spoil and rust on the stalk, and be wilted and threshed ere the harvest hath come!' It is sobering to turn from *Mardi* to *Pierre*, and to see how quickly Melville's sense of artistic promise turns into despair. But to think of the two books together is also to see more clearly the spirit in which *Mardi* is made. Of all his works *Mardi* is the one in which Melville's genius rejoices most unabashedly and unreservedly in its own powers. As no other novel in the world quite does, *Mardi* embodies the spectacle of a great author advancing, with perfect confidence and good cheer, to greet his own mature creative self.

—Richard H. Brodhead, "Mardi: Creating the Creative," *New Perspectives on Melville*, ed. Faith Pullin (Edinburgh University Press, 1978).

PLOT SUMMARY OF
The Confidence Man

The Confidence Man is a drastic change from Herman Melville's other novels. Much like Chaucer's *Canterbury Tales*, he introduces us to many characters traveling together, bonded by both their journey and a covert con game. The characters fall into two categories: those who are con artists and those who will be swindled.

The reader observes the comings and goings and conversations of the characters on board the *Fidele*, as if one is another traveler on the ship. Herein lies the difficulty of keeping the many characters straight. One reason for this difficulty is that Melville gives very few of his characters a proper name. Most of the characters are known by their description: such as the stranger in cream clothing, the black beggar, the herb doctor, and a well-to-do gentleman, to name a few. The entire story takes place on a boat traveling south on the Mississippi River. The travelers engage in very detailed and philosophical discussions while waiting for their destinations. Characters depart and more arrive aboard as the steam ship *Fidele* makes its scheduled stops along the river.

Most of the story is told in dialogue form between the characters. A wide variety of people are on board: beggars, scholars, and clergymen. Lack of confidence or trust in other people is the common theme that binds the characters together and creates the storyline for the novel. It's a subject that is as relevant to modern times as it was to the nineteenth century. As the Confidence Man gains the trust of another character, he gives that person a reason to lose confidence in mankind.

The story of the Confidence Man opens with a vivid description of a morning in April. The location is the Mississippi River in St. Louis, on a steam ship heading for New Orleans. A stranger in cream clothes is settling in for a trip and observes his surroundings and fellow passengers for the journey. A deaf mute is introduced, whose presence implies a greater significance in the story. The next character the reader meets is Guinea, the crippled black beggar. Some on board, including a man with a peg leg, believe Guinea is a fake. Guinea does not spend too much time on board, departing at an early port. He is mentioned throughout the story as the boat continues on its way.

Many other characters make notable appearances in the chapters. They debate, discuss and exchange tall tales to emphasize their points. The issue of Christian charity is one topic that is discussed. Some scholars say Melville used *The Confidence Man* to offer an opposite view of Ralph Waldo Emerson's 'New England' philosophy of thrift and self-reliance, rather than a more Christian 'love thy neighbor' approach to life. It's believed that the character Mark Winsome represents Emerson and Winsome's disciple Egbert is Thoreau. The discussions with these characters are used to find flaws in the transcendental movement.

Time passes on board the *Fidele*, but the progression of the journey is not the primary focus of the novel. The emphasis is on the dialogues between passengers, and the issues debated between them. While these dialogues are lengthy, they rarely offer insight into the characters themselves. They delve into several broad topics but do not offer any personal information about the characters, which makes it difficult to identify with the speakers. While there are many interesting points made during these debates, the characters themselves have short-lived stays.

The characters spend a great deal of money during the trip, ranging from a few dollars to hundreds of dollars. Some donate to alleged charitable causes, others are investing in their future, and still others (like the Barber) expect something in return for their services. In the barber's shop hangs a sign that reads 'No Trust,' which the Cosmopolitan finds very disturbing. In talking with the Barber, he learns that the sign was posted after customers avoided paying for haircuts and shaves. It is his way of making sure that he gets paid for services rendered. The Cosmopolitan tries to convince the Barber to have faith in his fellow man. He offers to pay the bill for any customers who do not pay. However, the irony is that the Cosmopolitan does not have enough money to pay the Barber for his shave and the 'No Trust' sign is put back up.

While many of the conversations do not add much interest to the story, a few stand out in Melville's quest to make a point. One such story involves the character of the Frenchman, who sees a play that inspires him to get married. He chooses his mate because he likes her 'liberal mould'—that is, her 'liberal education and equally liberal disposition.' It turns out that she is 'liberal to a fault.' He comes home one day in time to see a stranger leaving from their alcove.

Another tale shared by the travelers is that of the 'Indian Hater.' The story involves the son of a pioneer named John Moredock. Indians killed his entire family—his father, stepfather, mother, brothers and sisters. He spent his life avenging their deaths, hunting and killing the Savages responsible for his family's death. Even though he had an all-consuming hatred of Indians, he was a good father, neighbor and soldier. He had been a founder of the state of Illinois. He declined to become a candidate for Governor, because he would not negotiate treaties with Indians, as would be a necessary job requirement for the office. The lesson drawn from the story is that hatred and resentment can destroy one's ambition and religion.

Should a friend lend money to another? It's a debate that appears more than once in the novel. On at least two occasions, two friends discuss the possibility of a loan between them and the problems it might cause. The possible terms of the loan are mulled over during the lengthy discussion between one set of friends. One friend tells the story of a man named China Aster, a candle maker. One of China Aster's wealthy friends offers him a loan. At first, China Aster tries to refuse, but his friend's insistence wears him down and he takes the money. While things are fine at first, he does not invest the money wisely and it becomes a hardship to make payments on the loan. The friendship between China Aster and his friend erodes. He ends up taking another loan to cover the first loan, which still isn't enough to cover his debts. When it is time to pay back his friend, he does not have the money. China Aster dies a short time later ,and his wife loses her inheritance to pay his debts and has no way to support their children. The point of this tale is to demonstrate the problems of borrowing money from a friend. In the discussion between the two friends on board the *Fidele*, it is decided that it is best that friends do not lend each other money.

The story ends with the characters going to sleep. There is no concrete resolution as the Confidence Man continues to play his game. When the sun rises on another day, the Confidence Man will most likely scam another passenger. Melville ends the work with the line "Something further may follow of this Masquerade."

Many conversations take place on the *Fidele*, and it can be difficult to follow who is speaking: the con man or the victim. It is a bewildering world Melville creates, representing the reality he lived through—the rapid expansion of the United States, the changes from an agrarian to an industrial economy, and the social changes. *The Confidence Man* cannot be described as a conventional novel; it's best characterized as an on going, thought provoking exchange of ideas. It was the last book published during Melville's lifetime. *The Confidence Man* is drastically different from his other works, yet consistent in the fact that he challenges his readers.

LIST OF CHARACTERS IN
The Confidence Man

Black Guinea is a crippled man on board the *Fidele*, who is begging for money. Some on board think he is pretending. He leaves the steamer at an early stop.

Man with Peg Leg does not believe Guinea is crippled.

Episcopal clergyman questions Guinea about his plight.

Methodist clergyman is described as noble.

Henry Roberts is approached by the Confidence Man. He was advised of an investment opportunity with the Black Rapids Coal Company.

Man with the weed is how the character that talked with Henry Roberts is described in chapter 5. He is melancholy and speaks with a student nearby.

Man in gray coat and white tie asks for donations to the Widow and Orphan Asylum, recently founded among the Seminoles. He does speak kindly of Guinea to the clergymen. He tells a 'well-to-do' gentleman about his plan to create a worldwide charity to end poverty: if everyone in the world donated a small amount of money for a few years, they could collect a massive amount and the poor of the world could be cared for, forever. He does get money from a charitable lady for the widows and orphans.

Ruddy Man in traveling cap passes himself off as a representative of the Black Rapids Coal Company, and sells stock from his company to the collegian and the good merchant.

Herb doctor sells Omni-Balsamic Reinvigorator to Old Miser. He tries selling Samaritan Pain Dissuader to other passengers. A

Giant on board attacks him. He collects a donation for the Widow and Orphan Asylum.

Old miser buys Omni-Balsamic Reinvigorator from Herb Doctor.

Tom Fry, a former cooper from New York talks to Herb doctor, who gives him a remedy to try.

Dried up old man approaches Herb doctor. He tries to find 'Mr. John Truman,' the representative from the Black Rapids Coal Company, in hopes of buying stock. They cannot find him and believe Truman has left the ship. Herb doctor sells him a medicine for his cough.

Missourian talks to people about slaves and all the inventions being used to make work easier. This character is around for several discussions. He tells the tale of the Indian Hater.

Pitch distrusts all the young men who work for him. He believes all young men are rascals and are planning mischief.

The Cosmopolitan—Francis Goodman—or Frank is of average height and weight and is dressed in nice clothing, except for his inappropriate violet vest. He is involved in the Indian Hater conversation, and all conversations through the rest of the book. He needs money and asks for it whenever he has the opportunity.

Charles Arnold Noble—Charlie—is one of many 'strangers' on board the ship. He shares wine with Frank, who asks him for money. He is outraged and leaves.

Mark Winsome warns the Cosmopolitan not to see Charlie again. He introduces the Cosmopolitan to his disciple, Egbert.

Egbert is a disciple of Mark Winsome and explains the philosophy to the Cosmopolitan. The Cosmopolitan proposes that Egbert call him Frank, and the Cosmopolitan will call him

Charlie. The Cosmopolitan asks Egbert/Charlie for a loan. He tells the Cosmopolitan the story of China Aster.

The Barber has a sign in his shop that reads 'No Trust.' The Cosmopolitan goes in for a shave and convinces him to take down the sign and have confidence in his fellow man. The Cosmopolitan offers to pay for any customers who leave the shop without paying the Barber for his services. Ironically, the Cosmopolitan cannot pay for his shave. The Barber puts his sign back up.

Old man appears to be a former well-to-do farmer. He discusses the Bible with the Cosmopolitan.

CRITICAL VIEWS ON

The Confidence Man

WILLIAM B. DILLINGHAM ON CHARITY

[In this essay, Dillingham explains the influence of 'Christian Charity' in The Confidence Man.]

In the first four of the eight roles he plays, the confidence man makes his plea to humanity in the name of charity, the second virtue of self-awareness. The deaf-mute holds up to a suspicious public the words of Saint Paul on charity. Black Guinea plays this "game of charity," trying in a different way from the deaf-mute to get his fellows to taste the flavor of benevolence by throwing him coins. When distrust develops among contributors, a Methodist minister speaks out for putting "as charitable a construction as one can upon the poor fellow" (p. 13). In response, a bitter one-legged man argues heatedly that charity has no place among men. After Black Guinea disappears, John Ringman approaches a country merchant and asks for charity to aid him in his plight. With chapter 6 comes the man in gray, asking charity for the Seminole Widow and Orphan Asylum, but several "passengers prove deaf to the call of charity" (p. 28). Ironically, they are deaf whereas the deaf-mute can, in this sense, hear. The man in gray is successful, however, with others, including a clergyman; a gentleman with gold sleeve-buttons, to whom the collection agent describes his philanthropic scheme for a world charity; and "a charitable lady," who donates twenty dollars to the Seminole fund. In his last four roles, the confidence man makes his theme that of sound and rewarding investment. The representative of the Black Rapids Coal Company sells stock for greater wealth; the herb doctor sells investment in better health; the man from the Philosophical Intelligence Office asks his clients to invest in boys; and the Cosmopolitan argues repeatedly and lengthily for investing in humanity in order to escape the blight of cynicism and bitterness. In effect, however, what the Cosmopolitan is espousing is the same as that of the confidence man in his first manifestation, the deaf-mute, for charity and philanthropy are essentially the same virtue.

The degree to which the confidence man is successful in getting people to be charitable or to "invest" (in the larger and more humane sense) is secondary to Melville's wider purpose, which is to delineate the true nature of this virtue of charity-philanthropy as opposed to how the world often conceives of it and to link it with the development, understanding, and control of one's psychic forces. The mature, examined, and disciplined mind inevitably develops a benevolent stance toward humanity and poignantly intuits the necessity of such an attitude, but because that mind is so greatly superior to those of ordinary humanity, patience and kindness would be impossible without the quality that accompanies charity, namely a "saving" sense of humor. Humor, therefore, is an essential ingredient in *The Confidence-Man*, revealing the way in which the extraordinary man of self-knowledge deals with and retains his necessary connection with the world around him.

Melville obviously relies heavily upon Saint Paul's concept of charity, especially in chapter 1 when the deaf-mute writes five statements on his slate from 1 Corinthians 13: "Charity thinketh no evil," "Charity suffereth long, and is kind," "Charity endureth all things," "Charity believeth all things," and "Charity never faileth" (pp. 4–5). What is less obvious is Melville's use of another verse in that same chapter of 1 Corinthians: "When I was a child, I spake as a child, I understood as a child, I thought as a child: but when I became a man, I put away childish things." Paul is clearly linking the feeling and practice of charity to spiritual maturity and by implication charging those who lack true benevolence and long-suffering patience with being childish. Melville picked up on this association of charity with maturity and conveyed it in a scene charged with some of the most effective irony in the book. The deaf-mute is described as a child and treated as one by those aboard the *Fidèle* when in actuality he is a mature man of self-knowledge who has put away childish things, and they are mental and spiritual toddlers in the guise of adults. The deaf-mute's "cheek was fair, his chin downy, his hair flaxen," like that of an infant. He stands near a placard "offering a reward for the capture of ... an original genius" (p. 3), but it is he who is the original genius, even if he appears to be a babe. Toward the end of the book, Melville remarks that "the sense of originality exists at its highest in an infant" (p. 238). As such, the man in cream colors appears to be cut off, for one cannot communicate with him in the ordinary ways. He seems to have been recently born, to have come from a far place. And like a child in his innocence and helplessness, he is now and then jostled aside or impatiently abused by the adults around him. Yet their "buffets" are all "unresented" as he offers a lesson in charity and then, again like a small child or infant, goes off to sleep without caring much where. Resembling a toddler, he is constantly in the way, and two porters with a trunk almost run over him, but he accepts it all with "lamb-like" forbearance. Though considered a "simpleton," he is the opposite.

The reason that charity grows out of self-knowledge is not merely that the great and ordered mind senses its superiority to society in general and thus is moved to a feeling of pity but more fundamentally that such a highly developed and self-aware mind realizes that it has to exist among the ordinary and will become unstable without some connection with the world of common people. Therefore, an original person cannot long remain so in aloof isolation. One comes to value company, even though not of the highest order, as necessary for self-understanding. This is what the Cosmopolitan means when he tells Charlie Noble that there is "a kind of man who, while convinced that on this Continent most wines are shams, yet still drinks away at them; accounting wine so fine a thing, that even the sham article is better than none at all" (p. 162). He then compares the inferior wine with inferior company and draws a parallel between the drinker and a "good-natured" person who "might still familiarly associate with men, though, at the same time, he believed the greater part of men false-hearted—accounting society so sweet a thing that even the spurious sort was better than none at all" (p. 162).

But this is not to say that the confidence man loves each person he encounters. To feel a sense of charity toward humanity and to value the company sometimes even of false-hearted people is not to cherish or even to like every Individual. With few exceptions, however, the confidence man remains tolerant and friendly, perhaps even benevolent, toward those he meets. He can do so because they are as children to him. He sees what they are up to, what they want, and he plays with them, not as the Devil toys with the damned but as a good-natured mature adult talks with a child and, without letting the child know it, amuses himself by manipulating the immature (and often selfish) mind. Throughout, the confidence man is in this way amusing himself, but in a good-natured, not satanic, vein. When John Ringman tells the merchant, Henry Roberts, that he has "a hundred times" laughed over something that passed between them, he may be indulging in the kind of storytelling that adults frequently practice with children, but he nevertheless reveals that indispensable quality that is the companion of charity, a highly developed and mature sense of humor as opposed to that pseudohumor characteristic of the immature or sick mind.

—William B. Dillingham, *Melville's Later Novels* (The University of Georgia Press, 1986).

HERSHEL PARKER ON CHRISTIANITY

[Hershel Parker is a Professor Emeritus in the English Department at the University of Delaware. In this essay he takes a look at the role of Christianity in *The Confidence Man.*]

The Indian-hater story, as I read it, is a tragic study of the impracticability of Christianity, and, more obviously, a satiric allegory in which the Indians are Devils and the Indian-haters are dedicated Christians, and in which the satiric target is the nominal practice of Christianity.

If Shroeder has not "let more light into this book than any other critic," as Miss Foster says, certainly his use of literary cross-references "to locate the events of *The Confidence-Man* geographically and spiritually" is the most illuminating criticism besides her own. Briefly as Shroeder treats the Indian-hater chapters, he indicates convincingly the diabolic nature of the Indians and the god-like character of the Indian-hater. Colonel Moredock, says Shroeder, "has succeeded in locating Evil in its real home; there is no distortion in his vision of spiritual reality." But I would quarrel with Shroeder's conclusion that the only hope in this "dark book" is that "the triumph of the confidence-man is opposed and objectified, though apparently not negated, by an adversary of heroic proportions"—that is, by Moredock. And I suggest that Shroeder, while accurately formulating the terms of the allegory, has missed the ironic inversion of accepted values which is the basis of Melville's gigantic satire.

Pearce's article amounts to a general contradiction of Shroeder's conclusions. He denies that the Indians "are symbols of satanism," and argues from Melville's attitude toward real Indians that he does not use the Indian symbolically in *The Confidence-Man*. Pearce submits "that there is nothing but distortion in the Indian-hater's vision of spiritual reality," and denies that Moredock "functions as a kind of hero." The artistic function of Melville's version of the Indian-hater story—a version in which hatred is called a "devout sentiment" and the hater is praised—"is to be too violent a purge, a terrible irony." In Pearce's reading there is hope neither in the blind confidence of some of the passengers of the *Fidèle* nor in Moredock's blind hatred: "The blackness is complete."

Although agreeing with Pearce that the Indian-hater is in no sense a hero, Miss Foster finds that "in the Indian-hater chapters the Indian embodies allegorically a primitive, or primal, malign, treacherous force in the universe." Unlike Pearce, she distinguishes between Melville's attitude toward real Indians and his use of them as symbols. She takes exception to Pearce's "blackness": "Melville, though a pessimistic moralist in this novel, is not, I take it, a despairing one. Like many another moralist and writer of comedy, he is concerned to point out the dangers of both extremes." Reading the section as one of Melville's warning qualifications of "the cynicism and materialism of the main argument," she concludes that Melville "gives us an unforgettable picture of a society without faith or charity.... This is the alternative if we jettison charity—a world of solitary, dehumanized Indian-haters."

Despite Miss Foster's tactful mediation between Shroeder and Pearce and despite her own interpretation, major problems remain. Neither Pearce nor Miss Foster has adequately explored the implications of Shroeder's evidence that the Indians are diabolic. Nor has enough been made of the likelihood that in an allegory as carefully structured as *The Confidence-Man* the antagonist of the satanic Indians might be in some way religious. Then, Pearce's disgust at the praise accorded Moredock (disgust shared by any reader of the Indian-hating story as a literal narrative) has not been reconciled with Shroeder's claim that Moredock is the heroic adversary of the Confidence Man. The solution lies, I suggest, in taking the episode as allegory, as Shroeder and Miss Foster do, and in carefully identifying the elements of that allegory. Melville's opposition of the Indian-hater and the Indian constitutes, I believe, a consistent allegory in which Christianity is conceived as the dedicated hatred of Evil at the cost of forsaking human ties, and in which most of the human race is represented as wandering in the backwoods of error, giving lip-service to their religion but failing to embody it in their lives. The allegory is a grotesquely satiric study of the theme which Miss Foster calls the most obvious in the novel, "the failure of Christians to be Christian," and in the vein of *Mardi* and *Pierre* it is a study of the practicability of Christianity as Jesus preached it.

Both Shroeder and Miss Foster offer evidence for the identification of the allegorical significance of the Indians. Demonstrating that snakes in *The Confidence-Man* are associated with the Devil as in Genesis, *Paradise Lost*, and Hawthorne's works, Shroeder argues cogently that the coupling of the Indian and the snake at the outset of the Indian-hater story is a deliberate guide to the diabolic nature of the Indians. Never definitely calling the Indians Devils, Miss Foster observes that in Mocmohoc "readers will have recognized a type of the Confidence Man." She also suggests the possibility that "the Indian is something not so much sub-human as extra-human," and that by giving Indian containers for their wine bottles and cigars to the cosmopolitan and Charlie (the ordinary Mississippi confidence man who tells the Moredock story), "Melville meant to remind the reader that they are the Indians of the argument." The same function, I would add, is served by Melville's having the cosmopolitan ironically call his pipe a "calumet"—a peace pipe. Miss Foster agrees that Shroeder "demonstrates beyond question the diabolic and mythic nature" of the Confidence Man, but she does not pursue the allegorical associations of the Indians with Devils. Yet if the Confidence Man is associated with snakes and is the Devil, while Indians are associated with snakes and at least one Indian is "a type of the Confidence Man," then in Melville's allegorical geometry the Indians are Devils also.

Recognizing the Indians as types of the Devil of Christian literary tradition, we should reasonably expect the Devil's antagonist to be an earnest Christian. But Moredock, who dedicates his life to killing, hardly fits the ordinary conception of a follower of Jesus. The cosmopolitan (the last avatar of the Confidence Man) makes the obvious objection in professing himself unable to believe that a man so loving to his family could be so merciless to his enemies. Pearce in a similar spirit rejects Shroeder's interpretation of Moredock as the man who has located Evil in its real home. But repugnant as it is, the logic of the opposition demands that we see Moredock as a Devil-hating Christian, though one who does not live up to all of Jesus' commands. The outrageous irony that has escaped notice is that it is when Moredock is murdering Indians that he is Christian and when he is enjoying the comforts of domestic life that he is apostatizing.

—Hershel Parker, "The Metaphysics of Indian-Hating," *Nineteenth-Century Fiction* 18 (September 1963).

JAMES DUBAN ON FAITH

[In this essay Duban finds evidence of the influence of faith in *The Confidence Man.*]

Less skeptical, however, was George Bancroft, who, in "The Progress of Mankind" (1854), applauded the way "the course of civilization flows on like a mighty river through a boundless valley, calling to the streams from every side to swell its current, which is always growing wider, and deeper, and clearer, as it rolls along. Let us trust ourselves," he adds, "upon its bosom without fear; nay, rather with *confidence and joy*."[1] Whether or not Melville knew Bancroft's essay, *The Confidence-Man*'s description of "the dashing and all-fusing spirit of the West, whose type is the Mississippi itself, which, uniting the streams of the most distant and opposite zones, pours them along, helter-skelter, in one cosmopolitan and confident tide" (CM, 6) invokes the progressive attitudes that the book finally subverts. These attitudes resemble those in the opening issue of the *Democratic Review*, which foreshadows the concerns of *The Confidence-Man* by declaring democracy

> the cause of Humanity. it has faith in human nature. It believes in its essential equality and fundamental goodness.... It is the cause of philanthropy.... It is, moreover, a cheerful creed, a creed of high hope and universal love, noble and ennobling; while all others ... imply a distrust of mankind, and the natural moral principles infused into it by its creator.[2]

This celebration of democracy and human nature is crucial for our purposes because it closely approaches the liberal Christian assumptions satirized by William R. Weeks's *The Pilgrim's Progress in the Nineteenth Century*, in which a character named "Liberal" declares,

> [T]here is certainly something very pleasant in thinking of others as favorably as we can.... If a stranger comes to my house, and calls himself a pilgrim, I am unwilling to be suspicious of him, and by a severe scrutiny to give him reason to believe that I am disposed to think every man an impostor. I am rather disposed to treat every man as if I thought him honest, till he proves himself otherwise.[3]

Ample precedent, then, exists for the "fresh and liberal construction" (CM, 46) espoused by the Confidence-Man in gulling his victims into what Ernest Lee Tuveson describes as a creed of *tout est bien*, the substance of which "is that for millennia mankind has been laboring under a monstrous delusion: it has mistakenly thought that evil is integral to nature and that evil is ingrained in the human heart."[4] This view coincides with the Unitarian outlook that the Confidence-Man offers up in his glorification of human nature, in his rejection of "Saint Augustine on Original Sin" (CM, 109), and in his at least nominal disbelief in imputed sin (CM, 107). There is also a Unitarian ring to the Confidence-Man's remark that "each member of the human guild is worthy of respect" (CM, 171); indeed, "Men have as yet no just respect for themselves," claimed William Ellery Channing, "and of consequence no just respect for others."[5] The Confidence-Man's thoughts on the "final benignity" of "heaven's law" (CM, 84) and the possibility that "mankind ... present as pure a moral spectacle as the purest angel could wish" (CM, 103) bring to mind Arminian ideas about God's benevolence and the absurdity of depreciating moral virtue.[6] Satirized, too, as shown by current scholarship, are the liberal ideas of William Cullen Bryant, Theodore Parker, and Horace Greeley—as well as the bastardized forms of Christianity that Orestes A. Brownson came to think characteristic of the cults which had earlier captured his Transcendental sympathies.[7]

Of course, Melville also dramatizes how misanthropy can be just as harmful as naive liberal confidence and how a supposedly "true sight of sin" can sustain proslavery apologetics and perpetuate modes of historiography that justify the extermination of Indians.[8] Eve-handedly, however, *The Confidence-Man* shows that a failure to acknowledge depravity has serious practical consequences and important doctrinal ramifications for the liberal Christian outlook more generally characteristic of nineteenth-century *Fidèle*. To these concerns let us now turn in a discussion of the book's epistemological drama, which first undermines the foundations of liberal confidence in man's faculties of perception but which then shows many of the *Fidèle*'s company to teeter on the brink of both infidelity and philosophical skepticism because they willingly ignore whatever "moral evidence" is proffered them concerning the reality of evil.

To understand the impact of *The Confidence-Man*'s skeptical epistemology, recall how liberal Christian claims to regeneracy presuppose the mind's ability to distinguish truth. "To reject human nature and declare it unworthy of confidence," claimed Orestes A. Brownson, "is—whether we know it or not—to reject all grounds of certainty, and to declare that we have no means for distinguishing truth from falsehood.[9] Nineteenth-century progressivist and liberal religious thought generally embraced the assumption that "the progress of man consists in this, that he himself arrives at the perception of truth"[10] and that

> [t]o confide in God, we must first confide in the faculties by which He is apprehended.... A trust in our ability to distinguish between truth and falsehood is implied in every act of belief.... In affirming the existence and perfections of God, we suppose and affirm the existence in ourselves of faculties which correspond to these sublime objects, and which are fitted to discern them. Religion is a conviction and an act of the human soul, so that in denying confidence to the one, we subvert the truth and claims of the other.[11]

Indicative of Melville's familiarity with ideas such as these is the section of *Mardi* in which the Old Man of (Unitarian/ Transcendentalist) Serenia says, "[M]en's faculties are Oro-given"; in fact, his belief that "to do [God's] bidding, then, some new faculty must be vouchsafed, whereby to apprehend aright" (M, 626) may even echo Charming's remark, "To confide in God, we must first confide in the faculties by which He is apprehended." Yet *The Confidence-Man*'s dramatization of man's inability to detect fraud—a point mirrored in the book's evasive and often confusing form—shows human nature to be unworthy of confidence when judged in the context of rationalistic liberal criteria for regeneracy. Aptly, then, the Confidence-Man acts out the dictum, expressed earlier in *Pierre*, that persons who "slide into the most practically Calvinistic view of humanity ... hold every man at bottom a fit subject for the coarsest ribaldry and jest" (P, 232).

NOTES

1. Whitman, "Motley's Your Only Wear," *Brooklyn Daily Eagle* (1 April 1846), in *The Gathering of the Forces by Walt Whitman: Editorials, Essays, Literary and Dramatic Reviews ... Written by Walt Whitman as Editor of the "Brooklyn Daily Eagle" in 1846 and 1847*, ed. Cleveland Rodgers and John Black, 2 vols. (New York: G. P. Putnam's Sons, 1920), II: 96; George Bancroft, *Literary and Historical Miscellanies* (New York: Harper & Brothers, 1855), p. 516 (emphasis added).

2. "Introduction," *Democratic Review*, 1 (Oct. 1837), 11.

3. William R. Weeks, *The Pilgrim's Progress in the Nineteenth Century* (New York: M. W. Dodd, 1848), pp. 153–54. This hook was an expanded version of a

satire on liberal Christianity first published in the *Utica Christian Repository* (1824–26). See David E. Smith's informative chapter on Weeks in *John Bunyan in America* (Bloomington: Indiana Univ. Press, 1966), pp. 20–25. For the specifically Unitarian associations of the term "Liberal Christian," see Clarence H. Faust, "The Background of the Unitarian Opposition to Transcendentalism," *Modern Philology*, 35 (Feb. 1938), 311.

4. Ernest Lee Tuveson, "The Creed of the Confidence-Man," *English Literary History*, 33 (June 1966), 253.

5. Channing, "Honor Due All Men," in *The Works of William E. Channing, D.D.* (Boston: American Unitarian Assoc., 1895), p. 67.

6. See, for example, Charles Chauncy, *The Benevolence of the Deity* (1784); Jonathan Mayhew, *Two Sermons on the Nature, Extent, and the Perfection of the Divine Goodness* (1763); Lemuel Briant, *The Absurdity and Blasphemy of Depreciating Moral Virtue* (1749).

Melville's general familiarity with both the orthodox and liberal Christian traditions is suggested by his mother's membership in the Dutch Reformed Church and by his paternal grandfather's and father's Arminian and Unitarian leanings. See William H. Gilman, *Melville's Early Life and "Redburn"* (New York: New York Univ. Press, 1951), pp. 21–23, 38; Newton Arvin, *Herman Melville* (New York: William Sloane, 1950), pp. 30–35. Moreover, as Merton M. Sealts, Jr., shows, in *Melville's Reading: A Check-List of Books Owned and Borrowed* (Madison: Univ. of Wisconsin Press, 1966), item 496, in 1851 Melville acquired John Taylor's *The Scripture Doctrine of Original Sin Proposed to Free and Candid Examination* (1710), which became a primer for New England Arminians, later evoking Jonathan Edwards's *The Great Doctrine of Original Sin Defended* (1758). For further suggestions about Melville's familiarity with debates surrounding orthodox and liberal Christianity, see T. Walter Herbert, Jr., *"Moby-Dick" and Calvinism: A World Dismantled* (New Brunswick, N.J.: Rutgers Univ. Press, 1977), pp. 23–68.

7. See Helen P. Trimpi, "Three of Melville's Confidence Men: William Cullen Bryant, Theodore Parker, and Horace Greeley," *Texas Studies in Literature and Language*, 21 (Fall 1979), 368–95; Carolyn L. Karcher, "Spiritualism and Philanthropy in Brownson's *The Spirit Rapper* and Melville's *The Confidence-Man*," *ESQ: A Journal of the American Renaissance*, 25 (1979), 26–36. Of course, studies such as these presuppose the by now generally accepted view that part of *The Confidence-Man*'s satire is leveled at a specifically Emersonian variety of liberalism. See Egbert S. Oliver, "Melville's Picture of Emerson and Thoreau in 'The Confidence-Man,'" *College English*, 8 (Nov. 1946), 61–72; Elizabeth S. Foster, "Introduction" and "Explanatory Notes" to *The Confidence-Man: His Masquerade* (New York: Hendricks House, 1954), pp. lxxiii–lxxxii, 351–61.

8. See Carolyn I. Karcher, *Shadow Over the Promised Land: Slavery, Race, and Violence in Melville's America* (Baton Rouge: Louisiana State Univ. Press, 1980), pp. 217, 243; Joyce Sparer Adler, *War in Melville's Imagination* (New York: New York Univ. Press, 1981), pp. 111–32, esp. 119–21.

9. New Views of Christianity (1836), in *The Works of Orestes A. Brownson*, ed. Henry F. Brownson, 20 vols. (Detroit: Thorndike Nourse, 1882–87), IV: 34.

10. Bancroft, p. 484.

11. Channing, "The Moral Argument Against Calvinism" (1809), in *Works*, p. 462.

—James Duban, *Melville's Major Fiction: Politics, Theology and Imagination* (Northern Illinois University Press, 1983).

CLARK DAVIS ON THE LACK OF FAITH

[Clark Davis is an Associate Professor of English at the University of Denver. He wrote *After the Whale: Melville in the Wake of Moby-Dick*. In this section, he explains how Melville's loss of faith is at the center of *The Confidence Man*.]

Largely a set of variations on the theme of social faith, this compilation of conversations and tales presents a remarkably fictive world which, like *Pierre*'s Saddle Meadows, both senses and plays upon its existence as fiction. Unlike *Pierre*, however, the later novel toys with the relative deceptiveness of its characters, presenting as part of its fabric the misleading narratives these characters concoct as they attempt to convince their victims within the book and us as readers to believe in them. This repetition of the pattern of seduction—the attempt to consummate a relationship via the convincing or evocative power of language—becomes one of the book's basic structural components and indicates Melville's continued pursuit of large-scale structural fragmentation and the attenuations of Ahabian desire. Though the metaphysical pursuit finds its highest expression in the final pages of *Moby-Dick*, it is after *Pierre*, the short fiction, and especially "Benito Cereno" that such a search is reduced to an impotent and paradoxical desire to elicit and destroy "confidence" wherever it is located. No longer can the metaphysical quester hope to seduce the inscrutable into physical revelation; at best he can employ his now purely linguistic body in repeated, false rehearsals of the divine seductions he once attempted.

Coupled with the confidence-man's fictive reality, we find here both an impalpable "landscape" or physical setting and a body that is presented either as a misleading mask or as evidence of the broken and diseased world that reflects the quester's inner condition. Thus the deceptive and fragmented form of the novel finds its reflection in the deceptive and fragmented bodies aboard the *Fidèle*, while the book as a whole projects the failure of social and linguistic faith even as it attempts to seduce its readers into a confidence in its own constructions. In this respect, rather than presenting a reducible allegory of satanic soul-takings, *The Confidence-Man* reveals itself to be a book about the seduction of faith in a fictive world of bodily and linguistic decay.[7]

The world of the *Fidèle* shares with sections of *Pierre* the distinction of being among Melville's most completely fictive "landscapes." Each, despite various claims to the negative, presents a world in which the physical body that had been so much the center of books like *Moby-Dick* and even *Israel Potter* no longer exists in substance as flesh. Instead, the *prima materia* of these worlds, their foundation and irreducible matter, is the "stuff" of words, of writing and talking, of textuality and fiction. From the book's first sentence, in which the man "in cream colors" appears "suddenly as Manco Capac at the lake Titicaca," we realize that the setting of this novel of appearances and disappearances is of little concern to Melville.[8] Very few words are spent on description of anything other than the superficial trappings of the various passengers and those few details of the ship needed to give each dialogue the semblance of a location.[9] In fact, the first attempt to describe the landscape places us more in the realm of distant legend—"The great ship-canal of Ving-King-Ching, in the Flowery Kingdom" (8)—than it does on the currents of the Mississippi. Similarly, the other brief visions of the shore or river waters are equally evanescent, as though all background for the book's voices is seen through gauze or partially intuited by a nearsighted eye. Physical scenery passes in a blur, either "rapidly shooting" or "seen dimly" (8), and only the shapes of amorphous "crowds," "bluffs," and "shot-towers" (8), the largest units of descriptive cognizance, present themselves to the narrative vision.

The other "major" descriptive passages of the landscape similarly stress the unreality rather than the concreteness of this book's world. Both in their generality and in their figurative connections to the fictive, such "settings" offer us a consistently twilit universe regardless of the ostensible time of day: "The sky slides into blue, the bluffs into bloom; the rapid Mississippi expands; runs sparkling and gurgling, all over in eddies; one magnified wake of a seventy-four. The sun comes out, a golden huzzar, from his tent, flashing his helm on the world. All things, warmed in a landscape, leap. Speeds the daedal boat as a dream" (77). This sparkle and gurgle is the most Melville gives us of the water, once so significant and powerful an element in his books' worlds, while the land, always problematic and important in his earlier works, here simply "slides" by as though exhibited under glass. No colors appear except the sun's gold; what "things" it warms into leaping we have no way of knowing or seeing. Only the final sentence confirms what we have been too long suspecting: that this book is in fact, like the speeding boat, a construct, a "daedal" mechanism moving through the blurred figures of a dreamed world.

If the world in *The Confidence-Man* begins to betray its fictiveness by means of its impalpability, however, then the individual body reveals its own deceptive nature through the repeated appearance of diseased or crippled characters. Of those aboard the *Fidèle* who appear either sick or wounded, there are two primary groups: first, an assortment of passengers who either participate in the presentation of a society in decay or bear the marks of previous seductions; and second, those confidence-men who bear "false" wounds in order to deceive.[10]

Of the passengers, those who are both diseased and gullible, whose physical suffering forces them into strained acts of faith, serve as objects of prey and scorn to the confidence-man even as they remind us that the *Fidèle*'s humanity tends toward spiritual and physical failure. They carry the disease that often seems to inhabit the very air, a "Cairo" fever (129) of failed contact with the lost sources of spiritual health. The "shrunken old miser," for instance, whose dignity and health have been compromised by a commitment to material rather than spiritual values, is "eagerly clinging to life and lucre, though the one was gasping for outlet, and about the other he was in torment lest death, or some other unprincipled cut-purse, should be the means of his losing it; by like feeble tenure holding lungs and pouch, and yet knowing and desiring nothing beyond them; for his mind, never raised above mould, was now all but mouldered away" (58). The equation in this passage of "mould" with money, flesh with the decay of materialist values, reinforces the presentation of the individual who has sold life for lucre and whose body, approaching the static lifelessness of the money it so feverishly hoards, nears failure. Thus the mind "never raised above mould" has finally infected the body and so brought about a reversal of what has been for Melville a positive dialectic. Instead of the body's subsumption and resurrection of the often ethereal mind, here we have a mind, itself poisoned by a blind materialism, further tainting and finally destroying the flesh that was once the locus of its salvation. In this respect, the miser's subsequent seduction in chapter 15 simply reaffirms his failure to invest in some degree of transcendence, for even to the end he attempts to buy back the health that his devotion to money has stolen from him.

In contrast, the majority of the diseased or wounded victims aboard the *Fidèle* reveal varying degrees of such materialism combined with a cynicism or distrust whose strength depends upon the depth of their wounds. This list includes the man with the "wooden leg," the "invalid Titan," the "soldier of fortune," and the famously fictional Colonel Moredock. Though the histories of these characters are variously incomplete, they all enact essentially the same pattern: each has encountered a type of "confidence-man" in his past and now bears the scar of the wound to which his former trust made him vulnerable. Thus the body bears the evidence of seduction not because it was the target of the seducer but because it represents the social disjunction, the breaking up of the communal body that the failure of linguistic and social faith enacts. These characters are not only fragmented themselves; they are in fact the fragments of a world no longer connected by the invisible and vulnerable ties of social confidence, and they themselves reflect, ultimately, the splintering of the book's own form.

As the first of these walking wounded to appear, the "gimlet-eyed, sour-faced" (12) man with the wooden leg helps establish the basic type. Not only does he demonstrate the darkness of his cynicism in the episode with Black Guinea, but there is also the suggestion that he wishes to revenge an earlier blow. The narrator hints, for instance, that the "shallow unfortunate" could be "some discharged custom-house officer, who, suddenly stripped of convenient means of support, had concluded to be avenged on government and humanity" (12), while the "cripple" himself suggests that he may have been the victim of another kind of confidence. In telling the story of "a certain Frenchman of New Orleans" (30) who, having married a woman of a "liberal mould," fails to spot the most obvious signs of his cuckoldry, the cynic may in fact be rehearsing another version of his own loss of faith.

NOTES

7. Criticism of *The Confidence-Man* has come to mirror its subject's almost vertiginous complexity. However, it may be said, in general, that there are two basic approaches to the book and its central figure. The first attempts to identify the confidence-man in order to fix a full or partial allegorical pattern that will then help unlock the stubborn text. Among these, suggested identities include the devil, Christ, Christ-and-devil, the critic, a figure of self-knowledge, and a manipulator of fictions. Elizabeth S. Foster, Introduction to *The Confidence-Man: His Masquerade* (New York: Hendricks House, 1954); Daniel G. Hoffman, *Form and Fable in American Fiction* (New York: Oxford University Press, 1961), 279–313; Franklin, *The Wake of the Gods*, 177; Edward H. Rosenberry, *Melville and the Comic Spirit*, 153; Seelye, 121; Mushabac, 138; Dillingham, *Melville's Later Novels*, 306; and Roelof Overmeer, "'Something Further': *The Confidence-Man* and Writing as a Disinterested Act," *Études De Lettres* (1987): 43–53.

On the other hand, more recent readings have focused on the resistance of the text to any reading and have suggested that the confidence-man is a concealing author-figure, a type of the inconsistency of all character, a ventriloquist or deconstructor, or a combination of an allegorical and anti-allegorical figure. Dryden; Paul Brodtkorb, Jr., "*The Confidence-Man*: The Con-Man as Hero," *Studies in the Novel* I, no. 4 (Winter 1969): 421–35; Henry Sussman, "The Deconstructor as Politician: Melville's *The Confidence-Man*," *Glyph* 4 (1978): 32–56; A. Robert Lee, "Voices Off, On and Without: Ventriloquy in *The Confidence-Man*," in *Herman Melville: Reassessments*, ed. A. Robert Lee (London: Vision Press, 194), 157–75; and John Bryant, "Allegory and Breakdown in *The Confidence-Man*: Melville's Comedy of Doubt," *Philological Quarterly* 65, no. 1 (1986): 113–30.

—Clark Davis, *After the Whale: Melville in the Wake of Moby-Dick* (The University of Alabama Press, 1995).

JOYCE SPARER ADLER ON MELVILLE'S LOSS OF FAITH IN AMERICA

[Joyce Sparer Adler was a Professor at the University of Guyana and a college lecturer. She wrote *War in Melville's Imagination*. In this excerpt, she explains how

Melville has lost faith in the policies and politics of the United States, and his opinions are found in *The Confidence Man*.]

Although designed as a puzzle never to be completely solved, *The Confidence-Man: His Masquerade* (1857)[1] makes one thing indisputable: that by the time of its composition Melville had no faith that the United States would voluntarily see its ills and dangers. In his bitter state of mind in 1855–56[2] he looked at the "time and place" to which, in the first chapter, the Christ-suggesting figure and his writings seem "somehow inappropriate" and found what he saw to be hideous: lust—for money, for land, for a sense of power to gull others—had brought slavery, poverty, wars of expansion, the near extermination of the native "Indian" population, and was now leading to some great total disaster. As a result, and as if following the advice and example of Hamlet (who appears in a parenthesis that has the force of italics), he undertook to show "the very age and body of the time his form and pressure"; plotted to catch conscience by means of a play; and, in the spirit of Hamlet assaulting his mother, set up a glass before the country that would confront it with so repulsive a reflection of itself as to cause self-revulsion, make it repent the past, and "avoid what is to come." He seems from the concluding line of the work to have retained one grain of hopeless hope: "Something further may follow of this Masquerade"—the masque he had presented.

To give vent to his extreme feeling and to shock his readers into self-knowledge, he needed an extreme form of expression. Responding to that demand, his imagination created a unique variation of the grotesque, a language new in American literature. In structure, imagery, diction, in the conception of characters, situations, and dialogues, and in the narratives told along the way—above all in the much-misread story of the Indian-hater—the art of *The Confidence-Man* reflects the grotesque reality that Melville saw beneath the nation's masks.

In his nightmare vision, America assumes the shape of a Mississippi River steamboat, the *Fidèle*, hurrying downstream on a day of diabolical jokes toward and then past Cairo, the last place where there is still a chance to turn from the downriver course. The passengers, representing the nationalities and sections of the country, distrust each other but do not wonder about the state of the *Fidèle*. On this "ship of fools" (iii, 22) where each has his own self-deception, the shared delusion is that the ship is sound. "Speeds the daedal boat as a dream" (xvi, 105) on an April Fools' Day when all is chaos and values are "topsy-turvy."

The Confidence-Man is a jigsaw puzzle, demanding the putting together of countless descriptions, disguises, encounters, narratives, images, names, phrases, and other odd bits and pieces to form an overall picture. But even when most of the pieces are joined, the picture that comes together is and must ever remain partly mysterious, because its central figure, the confidence-man in his many roles, is never allowed to be clearly defined: the puzzle is intended to continue to work in the reader's mind, like the crippled "soldier's" powder in "the Happy Man" (xviii, 131). But the setting in which the central figure appears is sharply drawn, and this setting is the real subject of the work. The *function* of the confidence-man is almost openly explained in the fragment that is the key piece in the assembling of the jigsaw puzzle. He is the one whom Melville, under the pretense of denying it, conceives as a true "original character" in fiction, the one who "essentially ... is like a revolving Drummond light, raying away from itself all round it—everything is lit by it, everything starts up to it" (xliv, 330). Whatever his true character, "if any" (xli, 311) the confidence-man serves to test the true characters of the others. He casts his light on a confidence-man society.

Conflicts among people characterize such a society. Manhunting is inherent to it; love cannot exist in it. The picture developed in *The Confidence-Man* is of a masked war: the *Fidèle* resembles a "whitewashed fort"; antagonism among the passengers is featured in every scene and has its echo in the warring impulses within individuals. The *Fidèle*, conglomerating all kinds of misplaced or pretended faith, carrying creatures of prey and victims, is a representation of a psychologically, morally, intellectually sick society, destructive and self-destructive.

No wonder, then, that *The Confidence-Man* is filled with images of disease, alienation and self-alienation, decay, and death. No wonder the cast is composed of grotesquely conceived characters like the old miser whose head looks as if it has been whittled by an idiot out of a knot, who lies close to death but clings to "life and lucre," attracting to him flies lured by the coming of decay, his mind, too, all but moldered away; or like Goneril of cactuslike appearance who hates her husband and—going Shakespeare's Goneril one better—is jealous of her child; or like Moredock, the Indian-hater, who, even late in life, likes to go out for "a few days' shooting at human beings" (xxvii, 219); or like the misanthropic Missourian who, finding them the only ones who serve film well, considers machines the only true Christians and rejoices that the day is at hand when "prompted to it by law," he will shoulder his gun and "go out a boy-shooting" (xxii, 162); or like any one of the other symbolic cripples, invalids, and victims of obsessions of all kinds who people the work. No wonder the lamp of Christianity stinks at the end and the confidence-man blows it out as he leads the old man away to an unknown fate. In this critical time Melville's imagination had to work with such images. The mask of comedy that the work wears has a death's-head grin.

The macabre comedy begins at sunrise with the appearance on deck of a white lamblike figure, "in the extremest sense of the word, a stranger"; the carnival continues through the confidence-man's (and others') disguises; and it ends with him in his synthesized role as "the cosmopolitan," leading an old man out of the cabin while the others in it "who wanted to sleep, not see" lie dead to the world. In each of the confidence-man's appearances, Melville casts doubt on whether he is what he appears to be: the lamblike figure may be an "impostor"; Black Guinea, the beggar, may be a "white operator in disguise"; the cosmopolitan may be intending harm to the old man or saving him from the fate of those in the cabin; in every encounter Melville makes it impossible to define the boundary between the words that express the confidence-man's real thoughts and those that "start up" the one to whom he is speaking.

Among the motley collection of hypocrites, man haters, and fools whom the confidence-man encounters, two pretenders are of particular significance in connection with the chapters on the Indian-hater. The first is a wealthy gentleman with gold sleeve buttons who has a very "winsome" aspect (vii, 50–53); the adjective will become his companion-character's name. He wears a white kid glove on one hand, while the other hand, ungloved, is hardly less white. Melville marvels that hands can retain such spotlessness on the soot-streaked deck of the *Fidèle*. But the explanation is simple: the man avoids touching anything himself; he has a servant to do his touching for him, a man "having to do with dirt on his account." But if, says Melville, "with the same undefiledness of consequences to himself, a gentleman could also sin by deputy, how shocking that would be!" Then he adds: "But it is not permitted to be; and even if it were, no judicious moralist would make proclamation of it." The second character, linked to this one through the idea of sinning by deputy, is Mark Winsome (xxxvi–xxxvii, 265–80). He is a New England mystic philosopher, a caricature of Emerson, who sits "purely and coldly radiant as a prism," who seldom cares to be consistent, and who keeps his love of things "in the lasting condition of an untried abstraction." He, too, has a deputy who acts for him—Egbert, his "practical disciple" who reduces the principles of Mark Winsome to practice, a thriving young merchant, "a practical poet in the West India trade" who looks as if "he might, with the characteristic knack of a true New-Englander, turn even so profitless a thing [as mysticism] to some profitable account." So Mark Winsome, also, is one who has his ideas and questionable desires put into practice by another. The idea of acting by deputy serves as the main link between the sections featuring Winsome and the man with the winsome aspect and the section on Indian-killing.

The account of Moredock the Indian-hater, with its preface on the "metaphysics" of Indian-hating, is told to the cosmopolitan by an Alabamian, Charles Arnold Noble, who recounts almost verbatim what was told time after time by his father's friend, Judge Hall. On the surface this section of the book tells the history of the Indian-killer's war on the Indians as the judge has long "impressed" it on people's minds. Hidden in it (though really not too deeply) is Melville's own view. In his black humor in this section is implied the contrast between what he felt was the true history of the war on the Indian and the mask of "history" he has the judge blandly place over it.

Whatever the judge impresses on his hearers, the Indian in

this section is not what the all but unanimous opinion in the critical literature about this story would have him—Melville's symbol of Evil.[3] How can one disregard the contrast between the outrageous things Melville has the judge say, in a sequence of increasingly unrestrained remarks, and the matter-of-fact way in which Melville has him say them? To ignore Melville's extravagant caricature of the way American history is told and to fail to sense his anger at what that history has actually been is equivalent to reading Swift's "A Modest Proposal" without awareness of the contrast between its recommendation that the nourishment of the infants of the Irish poor be subsidized so that they might be sold as food for the English landlords and the matter-of-fact way in which that idea is put forward—equivalent to ignoring Swift's bitter attack on the history of English–Irish relations. To establish that Melville's Indian-hating section is, like Swift's essay, a masterpiece of grotesque art to expose the real history of a conquering people and a conquered one is the objective of the remainder of this chapter.

The story of the Indian-killer is told to the cosmopolitan by the one character in the book who is clearly false from the start (xxv, 196–97). Noble's clothes, which are finer than his features, his florid cordiality, the "fictitious" way his vest flushes his cheek, even his "too good to be true" false teeth are instant clues to his spuriousness; the reader must look beneath the mask of his words. It might be said of him, as Melville has him say of Polonius, that he is paralytic all down one side, and that the side of nobleness. (Melville's punning on Noble's name is frequent.) The story that he relates is all rumor, repetition, and rhetoric. This is, or should be, obvious from the moment Noble, responding to the cosmopolitan's request for a little "history" of Moredock the Indian-hater, says: "Well: though, as you may gather, I never fully saw the man, yet, have I, one way and another, heard about as much of him as any other; in particular, have I heard his history again and again from my father's friend, James Hall, the judge, you know. In every company being called upon to give this history, which none could better do, the judge at last fell into a style so methodic, you would have thought he spoke less to mere auditors than to an invisible amanuensis; seemed talking for the press; very impressive way with him indeed. And I, having an equally impressible memory, think that, upon a pinch, I can render you the judge upon the colonel almost word for word" (201).

It is significant that the story has already been three times called not a story but a "history," and the narration, when it begins, will associate it with other historical annals and records. The other narratives told in the course of *The Confidence-Man* are all referred to as stories; the biography of Moredock is introduced and then quickly underlined as a history methodically presented by one who judges what is to be impressed on impressible minds. It is history as adjudged by writers like Parkman, whose treatment of the Indians Melville strongly criticized,[4] or like James Hall, whose works Melville took off from.[5]

NOTES

1. Herman Melville, *The Confidence-Man: His Masquerade*, ed. H. Bruce Franklin (Indianapolis: Bobbs-Merrill, 1967). All page references that follow in the text are to this edition.

2. For an excellent summary of the facts known about the state of Melville's mind, health, and finances in this two-year period, see Elizabeth S. Foster's "Introduction" in *The Confidence-Man* (New York: Hendricks, 1954), pp. xx–xxiv.

3. The outstanding exception is Roy Harvey Pearce's view in "Melville's Indian-hater: A Note on a Meaning of *The Confidence-Man*," *PMLA*, 67 (1952), 942–48, and in the chapter "The Metaphysics of Indian-hating: Leatherstocking Unmasked" in his book, *The Savages of America: The American Indian and the Idea of Civilization* (Baltimore: The Johns Hopkins Univ. Press, 1953).

4. See Foster's "Introduction," p. xlviii, for Melville's expression of opinion in his review in 1849 of Parkman's *Oregon Trail*.

5. Excerpts from James Hall's writings appear in Foster's "Explanatory Notes" at the end of the Hendricks House edition of *The Confidence-Man*, pp. 334–38. It is necessary to go to the original for the chapter called "Indian-hating" in *The Wilderness and the War Path* (New York, 1846). The latter makes it most clear that the real Hall, though he regrets the situation in the West, was nevertheless an apologist for the white American's war on the American Indian.

—Joyce Sparer Adler, *War in Melville's Imagination* (New York University Press, 1981).

Daniel G. Hoffman on Social Criticism

[Daniel G. Hoffman is a Professor Emeritus at the University of Pennsylvania. He's written poetry and literary criticisms during his career. In this essay, he explains how Melville wrote *The Confidence Man* to be a criticism of society.]

In *Moby-Dick* the inner conflicts of the individual and the outer conflicts between the soul and its environment had been magnificently fused. His next two major efforts tried to deal with these problems singly. Emerging from the involuted ambiguities of *Pierre*, Melville turned from that too-personal narrative to one last attempt at a panoramic view of society. Every reader of *The Confidence-Man* is struck by the diminuation of the scale of character and action. The confidence man himself deprecates the mode of the book: "Irony is so unjust; never could abide irony; something Satanic about irony. God defend me from Irony, and Satire, his bosom friend." Now there is no mighty hero, no world-mastering whale, no tattooed savages. The great hunters of *Moby-Dick* are replaced, in irony and satire, by these lesser breeds:

> Natives of all sorts, and foreigners; men of business and men of pleasure; parlor-men and backwoodsmen; farm-hunters and fame-hunters; heiress-hunters, gold-hunters, buffalo-hunters, bee-hunters, happiness-hunters, truth-hunters, and still keener hunters after all these hunters.

Melville's main interest is in the last-named hunters. The only Ishmael we can find aboard the riverboat *Fidèle* is a frontiersman—a truth-hunter who, despite his truculent independence and strong mind, is nonetheless duped, as are all the other hunters, by the confidence man.

The balanced encompassing of all the antimonies of experience, which saved Ishmael in *Moby-Dick*, had not proved possible for Herman Melville in life. "Lord, when shall we be done with growing?" Melville had written Hawthorne just after finishing *The Whale*; "As long as we have anything more to do, we have done nothing. So, now, let us add Moby-Dick to our blessings, and step from that. Leviathan is not the biggest fish;—I have heard of Krakens." But this ebullience could not last. Hawthorne gives this account of Melville's state of mind five years later, just after writing *The Confidence-Man*:

> Melville, as he always does, began to reason of Providence and futurity, and of everything that lies beyond human ken, and informed me that he had "pretty much made up his mind to be annihilated"; but still he does not seem to rest in that anticipation; and, I think, will never rest until he gets hold of a definite belief. It is strange how he persists—and has persisted ever since I knew him, and probably long before—in wandering to-and-fro over these deserts, as dismal and monotonous as the sand hills amid which we were sitting. He can neither believe, nor be comfortable in his unbelief; and he is too honest and courageous not to try to do one or the other.[1]

In *The Confidence-Man* Melville wanders to-and-fro over the deserts of an American world in which humane values are impossible and divine laws remain shrouded in mysteries impenetrable to anyone aboard his "ship of fools." This is a despairing book, a bitter book, a work of Byzantine ingenuity. It is as though Melville, denied Ishmael's godlike power to grasp the farthest limits of life, tries, and tries, and tries to spin out of the knotted web of severely limited experience the furtive pattern of truth. In *The Confidence-Man* experience is severely limited—to the operations of a swindler on a riverboat, playing, it would seem, for low cash stakes. But each of his diddles demands "full confidence" of his dupe, and each is a "type" of the Fall of Man.

Despairing though it be, *The Confidence-Man* has a wry gusto that carries the reader over its vertiginous argument. Stylistically it is distinguished, and marks a radical departure from both the high rhetoric and the comic palaver of *Moby-Dick*. This style has a new satiric edge, sharpened by images as unexpected as they are apt:

> The miser, a lean old man, whose flesh seemed salted codfish.... His cheek lay upon an old white moleskin coat, rolled under his head like a wizened apple upon a grimy snowbank.

And there is a new rhythm, whose involutions, even in descriptive passages, dramatize the serpentine twistings of reason proposed by the confidence man:

> Goneril was young, in person lithe and straight.... Upon the whole, aided by the resources of the toilet, her appearance at distance was such, that some might have thought her, if anything, rather beautiful, though of a style of beauty rather peculiar and cactus-like.

What is given is taken away; what is removed, lingers. All is equivocal here.

The literary, philosophical, and cultural materials in this book are fused in so enigmatic a fashion that its interpreters have differed as to what the book is really about. Richard Chase, to whose study of Melville in 1949 we owe the discovery of its importance, called *The Confidence-Man* Melville's "second-best book." He sees it as a work of social criticism, drawing on mythical prototypes for satirical intensity. John Schroeder soon rejected Chase's thesis; he reads *The Confidence-Man* as a religious allegory, proving debts to Hawthorne's "Celestial Railroad" and to *Pilgrim's Progress*. And Elizabeth Foster, uncovering still other sources for her critical edition, finds the book to be a tightly organized satire on optimism in its successive historical forms: the Shaftesbury position, the utilitarians, the Deists' faith in Nature, and transcendentalism. Nor are the critics agreed as to the form of the book, although there seems general opinion that it is fiction, and a novel—whether satirical, allegorical, symbolist, or tractarian.[2]

NOTES

"The Confidence-Man: His Masquerade." From *Form and Fable in American Fiction* (New York: Oxford University Press, 1961) by Daniel G. Hoffman.

1. Melville to Hawthorne, 17 November 1851; Hawthorne, *The English Notebooks* (20 November 1856), ed. Randall Stewart (New York & London, 1941), pp. 432–3. Hawthorne was then American Consul in Liverpool. Melville, on the verge of a nervous breakdown, had sailed to England for his health.

2. Chase, *Herman Melville*, pp. 185–209; Schroeder, "Sources and Symbols

for Melville's *Confidence-Man*," *PMLA*, LXVI (June 1951), 363–80; Foster, "Introduction" to *The Confidence-Man* (New York, 1954).

—Daniel G. Hoffman, "The Confidence Man: His Masquerade." *Melville: A Collection of Critical Essays*, ed. Richard Chase (Englewood Cliffs: Prentice Hall, Inc., 1962).

Helen P. Trimpi on Meaning

[Helen P. Trimpi is an author and critic. She wrote *Melville's Confidence Man and American Politics in the 1850s*. In this excerpt, she discusses how and where to fine Melville's meaning of *The Confidence Man*.]

Is it possible that the entire gallery of characters may relate to a specific historical context? If so, where should one look for them? This, then, is the double-faceted problem that *The Confidence-Man* has presented for the last decade. What specifically is the book about and does it have an historical context that would illuminate both its themes in specific detail and the objects of its satire in their particularities?

The method that one uses to attack both these questions is one that is useful, if not essential, in trying to interpret any work of literature of any period. One examines the literary form of the work, tries to define it in its historical terms, and attempts to place it in a literary tradition known to its author by means of comparisons with its pertinent parallels and analogues. This approach should bring the reader or scholar—through both sympathy and understanding—as close to the author's own intentions as is possible.

What was recognized from the beginning about *The Confidence-Man* by its more sensitive readers was that it is a satire. That is, to use the Aristotelean definition of comedy as expressed in the *Poetics*, it is a comic presentation of man, or men, as worse than they really are, with—to add the Horatian moral intention—the aim of improving them. To place it more specifically within the tradition of literary satire requires an examination of the formal elements of the narrative—some of which have already been adumbrated in the description of it given above—and some comparisons of it to other examples of satire.

If we examine *The Confidence-Man* we find five formal elements in its composition: (1) the protagonist—the title-character (the Confidence Man)—is a shape-shifting trickster who assumes a series of personal disguises; (2) the narrative structure of the book is primarily episodic, in that it unfolds in a series of short repetitive scenes; (3) the main expository device is the use of dialogue; as in a stage comedy, the bulk of the book is dialogue; (4) the principal action—repeated over and over—is the action of a confidence man trying to trick a fool; and (5) the characters may all possibly be satirical caricatures of known public figures of the time.

In the body of literary satire that was available to Melville there are at least two traditions that might have offered models to him: the narrative and the dramatic traditions. Of these, the first, the narrative tradition, which offers such models as *Don Quixote* in prose, Pope's *Dunciad* in verse, and Swift's *Gulliver's Travels* in prose—to name only the most obvious—has proven less fruitful than the dramatic tradition of satire. Analogues much closer in structure and characterization to *The Confidence-Man* may be found in the various forms of stage comedy. For example, Aristophanes' comedies in antiquity display at least three of the formal elements of Melville's satire: dialogue as the main expository device, the principal action of knave duping fool, and caricature of contemporary men. Ancient comedy likewise displays considerable use of comic disguise. Similarly, the Latin comedies of Terence and Plautus use dialogue, exploit the dramatic potential of knave duping fool, and they satirize Roman types and perhaps individuals. In the English Renaissance, the comedies of Ben Jonson, written with classical models in mind, also display some of the same formal elements of structure and characterization.

However, closer than any of these stage models to Melville's book is the dramatic tradition of satire as it was currently available to him in English stage Pantomime and in its ancestor, the Continental commedia dell'arte (improvised comedy) as it might be known to him through literary essays and histories of the early nineteenth century. This kind of stage satire was a living theater—the most widely popular of his time—not only in America but in England, France, and Germany, where in fact he saw examples of it in his travels. Commedia dell'arte with its seven principal masks, as they were described by Isaac D'Israeli, the English essayist, and by other historians, offers model character types not only for the shape-shifting trickster but also for nearly all the characters in *The Confidence-Man*. The mask Harlequin, a clever, witty knave who customarily assumes a series of disguises, offers a model for Melville's main character, the Confidence Man, while the mask Pantalone, who was an elderly, foolish Venetian man of wealth, presents a model for Melville's series of property-owning antagonists to the Confidence Man, most of whom are deceived by him. Both these character-types were retained in English and American Pantomime, as Harlequin and Pantaloon. Moreover, this form of comedy offers models in its other masks (the pedantic Dottore, the blustering Capitano, the cynical Pulcinella and the innocent Pierrot) for most of the other principal characters in *The Confidence-Man*.[8]

Structurally considered, *The Confidence-Man* bears a striking resemblance to English stage Pantomime of the period. A Pantomime began, according to its historian David Mayer, *Harlequin in His Element*, with the silent enactment in a single scene of a serious tale, myth, or legend known to the audience. Similarly, *The Confidence-Man* opens with the mysterious appearance of the Deaf-Mute, his writing of his message, his rejection, and his disappearance from the scene. Pantomime, next, after the transformation of the hero of the "Opening" into the comic figure of Harlequin, proceeded in a series of short repetitive episodes to unfold the encounters of Harlequin with his antagonist Pantaloon—whose character had likewise been adumbrated in the opening scene as an antagonist to the main character. Likewise, *The Confidence-Man* unfolds in a series of episodes, in each of which the Confidence Man, like Harlequin, appears in a disguise and precipitates and guides the action of the narrative. In Pantomime, Harlequin consistently tricks his opponent Pantaloon. Likewise, in *The Confidence-Man*, Melville's protagonist in his various disguises, tries to obtain money, or trust, or both, from his antagonists, who are almost consistently characters who carry purses, as Pantalone characteristically did, are elderly, as Pantalone usually was, or otherwise resemble this traditional dramatic mask and his descendant Pantaloon. Again, like the Harlequin of both commedia dell'arte and of Pantomime, Melville's Confidence Man also tries to outwit other types of characters, who may be seen to be modelled on other masks. For example, Mark Winsome, the Mystical Master, is clearly based on the Dottore type, as are also the Episcopal Clergyman, the Methodist Minister, and, less obviously, the Collegian—all of whom are solicited by the Confidence Man. The Missouri Bachelor Pitch, who carries a rifle, and the Soldier of Fortune, Thomas Fry, are modelled on the blustering Capitano mask of commedia dell'arte and are similar to the military types that were represented in Pantomime of the period. Similar again to the characterization in this dramatic tradition, Melville's two most cynical characters, the Wooden-Legged Man and the Invalid Titan, who resist successfully the Confidence Man's solicitations, are modelled upon the cynical Pulcinella mask.[9]

Thus, in the three formal elements of a shape-shifting protagonist, of episodic structure, and in the pattern of knave duping or trying to dupe other type characters (who are regional or social variants of universal human types), Melville's satire has close analogues in a stage tradition that we know was available to him. Commedia dell'arte, although not alive in the forms in which it had existed all over Europe from the Renaissance until the end of the eighteenth century, was written about by Diderot in the *Encyclopédie*, where Melville may have read about it in his translation, by D'Israeli, whose literary works he owned, and by Thackeray and Lamb in popular essays. As noted earlier, its descendant, the Pantomime of English theater, was the most vital comic theater of his time. We have evidence of Melville's attending performances of Pantomime and of its competitors, the farces, "entertainments," or "comicalities" of the period, as they were called.[10]

For the fourth formal element discerned in *The Confidence-Man*—dialogue as the chief expository method—Pantomime does not offer a satisfactory model, since it relied only minimally on spoken dialogue and mainly on body action plus written placards. However, commedia dell'arte and other forms of stage comedy generally offer analogues to Melville's chosen method of exposition. Dialogue is, of course, the chief expository device of stage comedy generally.

For the fifth element of structure the stage tradition of commedia dell'arte and Pantomime offers an explicit and nearly unique model for satirical caricature of contemporary public figures through allusion, parody, and mimicry. One of its main characteristics and cause of its great popularity was that this kind of comedy did satirize contemporary well-known persons (domestic and foreign) and took its subject matter from contemporary customs, fads, topics of conversation, social and political events, fashions—in fact, anything in the contemporary world that might offer itself for humorous or critical comment. David Mayer's study of English Pantomime emphasizes the popularity of this kind of topical humor as the source of Pantomime's lasting success. Histories of the American stage, likewise, refer to American versions of Pantomime and of English farces as a kind of native commedia dell'arte, based on local and regional American variations of the generic or universal types that the masks represented.

Lastly, there existed on the New York stage while Melville was living in the city, a close theatrical analogue to his conception of the Confidence Man. As Johannes Bergmann discovered in 1969, John Brougham's farce "The Confidence Man," which derived its main character from a real thief, William Thompson (whose activities originated the term "confidence man"), was performed at William E. Burton's Chambers Street Theatre during the summer of 1849. This comedy was favorably reviewed in the *Literary World*, which Melville read and for which he did some reviewing in this period. We know of it only that it was probably based on Thompson's activities and on newspaper articles that applied the new term "confidence man" to other men engaged in politics, business, banking, and other fields.[11] We do not know whether Melville saw the farce, but the possibility remains that he knew of it and that it may have remained in his mind as the germ of a possible narrative satire on American types and individuals.

For the foregoing reasons it is possible, then, to place Melville's work in the dramatic tradition of satire—more specifically in that of the improvised comedy and of Pantomime—though it must always be kept in mind that it is not, in fact, written for stage performance. (It is probably most accurately termed, as it will be seen later, a "pasquinade"—a political satire). By locating the work in this literary tradition we are enabled to undertake the solution to the problems it still presents to its readers: what it is about and who are the objects of its satire. For if, like improvised comedy in the European tradition and like Pantomime and other comical "entertainments" in Melville's day, *The Confidence-Man* is about contemporary types and individuals and is satirizing contemporary public topics and events, it is to the contemporary scene that one must look to find its meaning and to interpret its satire.

NOTES

8. This discussion of commedia dell'arte and Pantomime in relationship to *The Confidence-Man* is based on Helen P. Trimpi, "Harlequin–Confidence Man: The Satirical Tradition of Commedia Dell'Arte and Pantomime in Melville's *The Confidence-Man*," *Texas Studies in Literature and Language*, 16 (Spring 1974), 147–93. Cf. Tom Quirk, *Melville's Confidence Man: From Knave to Knight* (Columbia, Mo., 1982), pp. 19–30.

9. David Mayer, *Harlequin in His Element: The English Pantomime, 1806–1836* (Cambridge, Mass., 1969), pp. 1–5, 24. Trimpi, "Harlequin–Confidence Man," pp. 162–67.

10. Trimpi, "Harlequin–Confidence Man," pp. 156–58.

11. Johannes Dietrich Bergmann, "The Original Confidence Man," *American Quarterly*, 21 (Fall 1969), 560–77.

—Helen P. Trimpi, *Melville's Confidence Man and American Politics in the 1850s* (The Connecticut Academy of Arts and Sciences, 1987).

TOM QUIRK ON MELVILLE'S CHARACTER CREATION

[Tom Quirk is a Professor of English at the University of Missouri. He wrote *Melville's Confidence Man: From Knave to Knight*, *Nothing Abstract: Investigations in the American Literary Imagination*, *Coming to Grips with Huckleberry Finn*, and *Mark Twain: A Study in the Short*

Fiction. In this section, he studies how Melville created the title character.]

For this reason the title figure played a particularly significant role in the development of Melville's narrative. Not only did the confidence man inspire his subject, but the created character based on him might provide a structural principle as well, one that could connect and give coherence to otherwise discrete and unrelated episodes. The experience of writing *Israel Potter* had taught Melville that a central character could be used in this way, but by the time he came to have his confidence man masquerade as the cosmopolitan, his ambition for the character had transcended its original, narrowly satirical, and conveniently structural function, and he ultimately sought to create a truly original character in the figure of the cosmopolitan.

In the title of chapter 44, Melville playfully and ambiguously suggests that this chapter "will be sure of receiving more or less attention from those readers who do not skip it" (238). Not many critics of the book have skipped this chapter, but perhaps they have not given it the necessary "careful perusal" (a phrase Melville used in an earlier draft of the chapter title). It is, in fact, a chapter about original characters and his own attempt to create one in the figure of the cosmopolitan, though it masquerades as a discursive explanation of why the application of the phrase *quite an original* to the cosmopolitan is ill advised.

"True, we sometimes hear," he wrote, "of an author who, at one creation, produces some two or three score such characters; it may be possible. But they can hardly be original in the sense that Hamlet is, or Don Quixote, or Milton's Satan. That is to say, they are not, in a thorough sense, original at all. They are novel, or singular, or striking, or captivating, or all four at once" (238). That Melville should balk at the suggestion that a novel might contain any number of new or original characters is to his credit. When one recalls the admirably drawn figures that fill the pages of *The Confidence-Man*—Pitch, the Missouri bachelor; Charlie Noble, the Mississippi operator; Black Guinea; the Titan; Egbert; and Mark Winsome—it is evident that Melville could populate his fiction with memorable characters easily enough.

But apparently he did not believe they possessed anything more than a certain "striking" quality. Nor, finally, could he claim true originality for even the most interesting character in the book, Frank Goodman, the cosmopolitan. The supposed purpose of chapter 44 is to show that that character is undeserving of the descriptive phrase *quite an original.*

Yet the fact that he compared his character to such original creations as those of Shakespeare, Cervantes, and Milton testifies to his high ambitions for him. What may well have begun as the impulse to explore the significance of his character and through him to fashion a simple strategy for connecting discrete satirical episodes obviously changed in the course of writing. The subordination of dramatic effects to a prominent central character seems to be what Melville had in mind when he compared original characters such as Hamlet to a Drummond light, which "rays away from itself" and lights all that comes within its sphere.

This chapter has obvious reference to Melville's own created character and his highest aspirations for it. Even discounting, as the narrator insists we do, for the failure of Goodman to rival true originals, the achievement is still impressive. From the moment Frank Goodman makes his appearance with the words "A penny for your thoughts, my fine fellow" (130), our attention is focused on a character whose identity and motives are mysterious to us, yet who is altogether fascinating and complete. This is not to say that the confidence man in his other manifestations is not "striking" or "singular," but it is in the cosmopolitan that Melville strove to create a true original. As we shall see, the confidence man in his previous disguises is often derivative and serves in the main as a satirical vehicle, not as a figure with whom its creator might easily identify. The cosmopolitan, on the other hand, often serves as a spokesman for Melville's own deeply held convictions and at times represents the author's feelings toward his own situation. Moreover, that character is largely the result of the author's attempts to emulate the creators of those original characters he names in chapter 44, each of whom exerted his peculiar influence upon the formation of Frank Goodman.

Melville may have succeeded better than he knew in creating

a character that, in all of its disguises, "rays away from itself all around it." As Warner Berthoff has asserted, the final importance of *The Confidence-Man* is the "catholicity of its reach":

> not only that it spans a broad range of occasions and analogous further concerns. With a vividness of emphasis that seems, as we observe it, to surprise life itself, the thrust of imagination in *The Confidence-Man creates*—according to the angle and mass of its local attack—the very scenes it so solidly particularizes.

Which is to say that those very "significances" Melville found in his material had an urgency of interest and breadth of application that he effectively dramatized by the very situation the confidence man himself creates.

—Tom Quirk, *Melville's Confidence Man: From Knave to Knight* (University of Missouri Press, 1982).

WORKS BY

Herman Melville

Typee: A Peep at Polynesian Life; The Story of Toby, 1846.

Omoo: A Narrative of Adventures in the South Seas, 1847.

Mardi: and a Voyage Thither; *Redburn: His first Voyage*, 1849

White Jacket; or The World in a Man-of-War, 1850.

Moby Dick, 1851.

Pierre, or The Ambiguities, 1852.

Israel Potter: His Fifty Years of Exile, 1855.

The Piazza Tales, including "Bartleby the Scrivener" and "Benito Cereno", 1856.

The Confidence Man: His Masquerade, 1857.

Battle-Pieces and Aspects of War, 1866.

Clarel: A Poem and Pilgrimage in the Holy Land, 1876.

John Marr and Other Sailors, 1888.

Timoleon, 1891.

Billy Budd, 1924.

WORKS ABOUT

Herman Melville

Adamson, Joseph. *Melville, Shame and the Evil Eye: A Psychoanalytic Reading*. Albany: State University of New York Press, 1997.

Anderson, Charles Roberts. *Melville in the South Seas*. New York: Columbia University Press, 1939.

Arvin, Newton. *Herman Melville*. New York: Viking Press, 1957.

Baird, James R. *Ishmael.* Baltimore: Johns Hopkins University Press, 1956.

Bernstein, John. *Pacifism and Rebellion in the Writings of Herman Melville*. The Hague: Mouton, 1964.

Bickley, R. Bruce, Jr. *The Method of Melville's Short Fiction.* Durham: Duke University Press, 1975.

Bloom, Harold, ed. *Major Literary Characters: Ahab*. New York: Chelsea House Publishers, 1991

———. *Modern Critical Views: Herman Melville*. New York: Chelsea House Publishers, 1986.

Borton, John. *Herman Melville: The Philosophical Implications of Literary Technique in Moby Dick*. Amherst, MA: Amherst College Press, 1961.

Brodhead, Richard H., ed. *New Essays on Moby Dick*. Cambridge, England: Cambridge University Press, 1986.

Brown, Ray B. *Melville's Drive to Humanism*. Lafayette, Ind.: Purdue University Studies, 1971.

Chase, Richard, ed. *Melville: A Collection of Critical Essays.* Englewood Cliffs, N.J.: Prentice Hall, 1964.

Cohen, Bainard. *Exiled Waters: Moby-Dick and the Crisis of Allegory*. Baton Rouge: Louisiana State University Press, 1982.

Cohen, Hennig, ed. *The Battle-Pieces of Herman Melville*. New York: Thomas Yoseloff, 1963.

Davis, Clark. *Moby-Dick*. Tuscaloosa: The University of Alabama Press, 1995.

Davis, Merrell R. *Melville's Mardi: A Chartless Voyage*. New Haven: Yale University Press, 1952.

Dillingham, William B. *An Artist in the Rigging: The Early Work of Herman Melville*. Athens: University of Georgia Press, 1972.

Dillingham, William B. *Melville's Later Novels*. Athens and London: University of Georgia Press, 1986.

Duban, James. *Melville's Major Fiction*. Dekalb: Northern Illinois University Press, 1983.

Ellis, R. *Men and Whales*. New York: Knopf, 1991.

Franklin, H. Bruce. *The Wake of the Gods: Melville's Mythology*. Stanford, California: Stanford University Press, 1963

Friedrich, Gerhard. *In Pursuit of Moby Dick*. Wallingford, PA: Pendle Hill, 1958.

Gilman, William H. *Melville's Early Life and Redburn*. New York: New York University Press, 1951.

Hardwick, Elizabeth. *Herman Melville*. New York: Viking Penguin, 2000.

Herbert, T. Walter. *Moby-Dick and Calvinism*. New Brunswick, N.J.: Rutgers University Press, 1977.

Hetherington, Hugh W. *Melville's Reviewers: British and American, 1846-1891*. Chapel Hill: University of North Carolina Press, 1961.

Hillway, Tyrus. *Herman Melville*. Boston: Twayne Publishers, 1979.

James, C.L.R. *Mariners, Renegades and Castaways*. New York: James, 1953.

Kelley, Wyn. *Melville's City: Literary and Urban Form in Nineteenth-Century New York*. Cambridge, UK: Cambridge University Press, 1996.

Lebowitz, Alan. *Progress into Silence: A Study of Melville's Heroes.* Bloomington: Indiana University Press, 1970.

Mason, Ronald. *The Spirit above the Dust: A Study of Herman Melville*. London: John Lehmann, 1951.

Metcalf, Eleanor Melville. *Herman Melville: Cycle and Epicycle.* Cambridge, Mass.: Harvard University Press, 1953.

Olson, Charles. *Call Me Ishmael.* New York: Harcourt, Brace, 1947.

Parker, Hershel. *Herman Melville: A Biography Volume 1, 1819-51.* Baltimore: Johns Hopkins University Press, 1996.

Percival, M.O. *A Reading of Moby Dick*. Chicago: University of Chicago Press, 1950.

Pullin, Faith, ed. *New Perspectives on Melville*. Kent, Ohio: Kent State University Press, 1978

Quirk, Tom. *Melville's Confidence Man: From Knave to Knight.* Columbia, Missouri: University of Missouri Press, 1982.

Rogin, Michael Paul. *Subversive Genealogy: The Politics and Art of Herman Melville*. New York: Knopf, 1983.

Rosenberry, Edward H. *Melville*. London: Routledge & Kegan Paul, 1979.

———. *Melville and the Comic Spirit*. Cambridge, Mass.: Harvard University Press. 1955.

Sedgwick, William Ellery. *Herman Melville, The Tragedy of Mind.* Cambridge, Mass.: Harvard University Press, 1945.

Selye, John. *Melville: The Ironic Diagram*. Evanston: Northwestern University Press, 1970.

Severin, Tim. *In Search of Moby Dick: The Quest for the White Whale*. New York: Basic Books, 2000.

Sparer Adler, Joyce. *War in Melville's Imagination*. New York: New York University Press, 1981.

Stefoff, Rebecca. *Herman Melville*. New York: Julian Messner, 1994.

Sten, Christopher. *Sounding the Whale: Moby-Dick as Epic Novel.* Kent, Ohio: The Kent State University Press, 1996.

Thomson, Shawn. *The Romantic Architecture of Herman Melville's Moby-Dick.* Madison, NJ: Farleigh Dickinson University Press, 2001.

Trimpi, Helen P. *Melville's Confidence Man and American Politics in the 1850s.* Hamden, Connecticut: The Connecticut Academy of Arts and Sciences, 1987.

Wenke, John. *Melville's Muse: Literary Creation & the Forms of Philosophical Fiction.* Kent, Ohio: The Kent State University Press, 1995.

Zoellner, Robert. *The Salt-Sea Mastodon.* Berkley: University of California Press, 1973.

ACKNOWLEDGMENTS

"'Introduction' to *Moby-Dick*," by Alfred Kazin. From *Melville: A Collection of Critical Essays*, ed. Richard Chase (Englewood Cliffs: Prentice Hall, Inc., 1962): pp. 39–40. Originally published in the Riverside Edition of *Moby-Dick* (Boston: Houghton Mifflin Company, 1950, Riverside Ag), edited by Alfred Kazin. © 1956 by Alfred Kazin. Reprinted by permission.

"Melville and *Moby-Dick*," by Richard Chase. From *Melville: A Collection of Critical Essays*, ed. Richard Chase (Englewood Cliffs: Prentice Hall, Inc., 1962): pp. 49–50. Originally published in the Riverside Edition of *Moby-Dick* (Boston: Houghton Mifflin Company, 1950, Riverside Ag), edited by Alfred Kazin. © 1956 by Alfred Kazin. Reprinted by permission.

"Ishmael: The Nature and Forms of Despair," by Paul Brodtkorb, Jr. From *Ishmael's White World* (Yale University Press, 1965) 91–94. © 1965 by Yale University Press. Reprinted by permission.

Call Me Ishmael by Charles Olson (City Lights Books, 1947). © 1947 by Charles Olson, City Lights Books. Reprinted by permission.

"Ahab's Name: A Reading of the Symphony," by P. Adams Sitney. From *Modern Critical Views: Herman Melville*, ed. Harold Bloom (New York: Chelsea House Publishers, 1986): pp. 223–226. © 1985 by P. Adams Sitney. Reprinted by permission.

"A Thing Writ in Water: Allan Melville's Epitaph," by Neal L. Tolchin. From *Mourning, Gender, and Creativity in the Art of Herman Melville* (New Haven: Yale University Press, 1988): pp. 117–37. © 1988 by Yale University Press. Reprinted by permission.

Reprinted by permission of the publisher from "Incomparable America" in *The Culture of Redemption* by Leo Bersani, pp. 136–154, Cambridge, Mass.: Harvard University Press, © 1990 by the President and Fellows of Harvard College.

The Romantic Architecture of Herman Melville's Moby-Dick by Shawn Thomson (Madison, NJ: Farleigh Dickinson University Press, 2001): pp. 179–182. © 2001 by Associated University Presses. Reprinted by permission.

Sounding the Whale: Moby-Dick as Epic Novel by Christopher Sten (Kent, Ohio: The Kent State University Press, 1996): pp. 5–8. © 1996 by The Kent State University Press. Reprinted with permission of The Kent State University Press.

Exiled Waters: Moby-Dick and the Crisis of Allegory by Bainard Cowan (Baton Rouge: Louisiana State University Press, 1982): pp. 175–178. © 1982 by Louisiana State University Press. Reprinted by permission.

An Artist in the Rigging: The Early Work of Herman Melville by William B. Dillingham (Athens, GA: University of Georgia Press, 1972): pp. 136–139. © 1972 by the University of Georgia Press. Reprinted by permission.

Melville's Muse: Literary Creation & the Forms of Philosophical Fiction by John Wenke (Kent, Ohio: The Kent State University Press, 1995): pp. 168-170. © 1995 by The Kent State University Press. Reprinted with permission of The Kent State University Press.

The Wake of Gods: Melville's Mythology by H. Bruce Franklin (Stanford: Stanford University Press, 1963): pp. 99-103, 153-154, 179–180. © 1963 by Stanford University Press. Reprinted by permission.

Melville's Major Fiction: Politics, Theology and Imagination by James Duban (Dekalb, Illinois: Northern Illinois University Press, 1983): pp. 150–154, 192–196. © 1983 by Northern Illinois University Press. Reprinted by permission.

Reprinted by permission of the publisher from *Melville and the Comic Spirit* by Edward H. Rosenberry, Cambridge, Mass.: Harvard University Press, © 1955 by the President and Fellows of Harvard College.

"The Entangled Text: *Pierre* and the Problem of Reading," by Edgar A. Dryden. From *Boundary 2, 3*, vol. 7 (1979). Copyright © 1979 by *Boundary 2*. Reprinted by permission.

James, C.R.L. excerpts from Mariners, Renegades and Castaways: *The Story of Herman Melville and the World We Live In*, pp. 100–105 © 1953, 1978 by C.R.L. James, reprinted with permission of the University Press of New England.

Melville's City: Literary and Urban Form in Nineteenth-Century New York by Wyn Kelley (Cambridge, UK: Cambridge University Press, 1996): pp. 147–150. © 1996 by Cambridge University Press. Reprinted by permission of Cambridge University Press.

"Mardi: Creating the Creative," by Richard H. Brodhead. From New Perspectives on Melville, ed. Faith Pullin. © 1978 by Edinburgh University Press. Reprinted by permission.

"The Metaphysics of Indian-Hating," by Hershel Parker. From *Nineteenth Century Liturature*, vol. 18, no. 2 (1963): pp. 165–173. © 1963 by The Regents of the University of California. Reprinted by permission.

After the Whale: Melville in the Wake of Moby Dick by Clark Davis (Tuscaloosa: The University of Alabama Press, 1995): pp. 90–93. © by The University of Alabama Press. Reprinted by permission.

War in Melville's Imagination by Joyce Sparer Adler (New York: New York University Press, 1981): pp. 112–116. © 1981 by the New York University Press. Reprinted by permission.

"The Confidence Man: His Masquerade," by Daniel G. Hoffman. From *Melville: A Collection of Critical Essays*, ed. Richard Chase (Englewood Cliffs: Prentice Hall, Inc., 1962): pp. 125–127. From the Riverside Edition of *Moby-Dick* (Boston: Houghton Mifflin Company, 1950, Riverside Ag), edited by Alfred Kazin. © 1956 by Alfred Kazin. Reprinted by permission.

Melville's Confidence Man and American Politics in the 1850s by Helen P. Trimpi (Hamden, Connecticut: The Connecticut Academy of Arts and Sciences, 1987): pp. 5–9. © 1987 by The Connecticut Academy of Arts and Sciences. Reprinted by permission.

Reprinted from *Melville's Confidence Man: From Knave to Knight* by Tom Quirk, by permission of the University of Missouri Press. © 1982 by the Curators of the University of Missouri.

INDEX OF

Themes and Ideas